Assessing Russia's Decline

Trends and Implications for the United States and the U.S. Air Force

Olga Oliker • Tanya Charlick-Paley

Prepared for the

United States Air Force

Approved for Public Release; Distribution Unlimited

RAND

Project AIR FORCE

The research reported here was sponsored by the United States Air Force under Contract F49642-01-C-0003. Further information may be obtained from the Strategic Planning Division, Directorate of Plans, Hq USAF.

Library of Congress Cataloging-in-Publication Data

Oliker, Olga.
    Assessing Russia's decline : trends and implications for the United States and the U.S. Air Force / Olga Oliker, Tanya Charlick-Paley.
      p. cm.
    "MR-1442."
    Includes bibliographical references.
    ISBN 0-8330-3095-7
    1. Russia (Federation)—Strategic aspects. 2. United States. Air Force. I. Charlick-Paley, Tanya, 1968– II. Title.

UA770 .O43 2002
947.086—dc21

                                      2002073448

RAND is a nonprofit institution that helps improve policy and decisionmaking through research and analysis. RAND® is a registered trademark. RAND's publications do not necessarily reflect the opinions or policies of its research sponsors.

Cover design by Stephen Bloodsworth

Published 2002 by RAND
1700 Main Street, P.O. Box 2138, Santa Monica, CA 90407-2138
1200 South Hayes Street, Arlington, VA 22202-5050
201 North Craig Street, Suite 202, Pittsburgh, PA 15213-1516
RAND URL: http://www.rand.org/
To order RAND documents or to obtain additional information, contact Distribution Services: Telephone: (310) 451-7002; Fax: (310) 451-6915; Email: order@rand.org

In a post–Cold War world of great uncertainty, one of the least certain factors is the future of one of its two antagonists. Trends in the Russian Federation are not entirely negative, but there is cause for concern in the political, economic, demographic, and military realm, as well as continuing concern about the safety and security of Russia's civilian and military nuclear/industrial sectors. These trends should be cause for worry not only within Russia itself but also for the United States, for they increase the potential for instability and unrest in and relating to the Russian Federation, which creates dangers to the United States that, while entirely different, are no less serious than those presented by the Soviet Union in decades past. Russia's size, location, and nuclear arsenal guarantee that it will remain of vital interest to the United States for the indefinite future.

This study examines the form, extent, and implications of several of these trends and identifies their effects on U.S. interests generally and those of the Air Force in particular. It advances several notional scenarios for crises in and near Russian territory that threaten vital U.S. interests and considers how these scenarios might develop. Finally, it recommends steps the United States and its Air Force could take both to help limit the extent of Russian deterioration and to enable a better response to crisis should it occur.

This research was conducted in the Strategy and Doctrine Program of Project AIR FORCE under the sponsorship of the Deputy Chief of Staff for Air and Space Operations, U.S. Air Force (AF/XO), and the Director of Strategic Planning, U.S. Air Force (AF/XPX). It was part of a larger study, "New Challenges for the U.S. Air Force," which reviews "off-baseline" scenarios and threats—those receiving little attention in the defense community—for the purpose of identifying weak links in potential U.S. Air Force operations. Project staff are concurrently examining potential vulnerabilities and remedies in the deployment and employment of aerospace forces.

This report should be of interest to the national security community and members of the general public concerned with the future of Russia and Russian-U.S. relations. Comments are welcome and should be sent to the authors or to the overall project leader, David Shlapak.

PROJECT AIR FORCE

Project AIR FORCE, a division of RAND, is the United States Air Force's Federally Funded Research and Development Center (FFRDC) for studies and analyses. It provides the Air Force with independent analyses of policy alternatives affecting the development, employment, combat readiness, and support of current and future aerospace forces. Research is performed in four programs: Aerospace Force Development; Manpower, Personnel, and Training; Resource Management; and Strategy and Doctrine.

CONTENTS

FIGURES

What challenges does today's Russia pose for the U.S. Air Force and the U.S. military as a whole? Certainly Russia cannot present even a fraction of the threat the Soviet monolith posed and for which the United States prepared for decades. Yet, if certain negative trends continue, they may create a new set of dangers that can in some ways prove even more real, and therefore more frightening, than the far-off specter of Russian attack ever was.

As a weak state, Russia shares some attributes with "failed" or "failing" states, which the academic literature agrees increase the likelihood of internal and interstate conflict and upheaval. Tracing through the specifics of these processes in Russia reveals a great many additional dangers, both humanitarian and strategic. Moscow's efforts to reassert central control show that much control is already lost, perhaps irretrievably. This is manifested both in center-periphery relations and in the increasing failure of law and order throughout the country, most clearly seen in the increasing institutionalization of corruption and crime.

Although Russia's weakened armed forces are unlikely, by temperament and history, to carry out a coup, real concerns exist that the forces may grow less inclined to go along with aspects of government policy, particularly if they are increasingly used as instruments of internal control as in Chechnya. Moreover, the fact that the Russian military is unlikely to attempt to take power does not mean that it will not seek to increase its influence over policymaking and policymakers. The uncertainties of military command and control threaten the possibility of accidental (or intentional) nuclear weapon use, while deterioration in the civilian nuclear sector increases the risk of a tragic accident.

Russia's demographic trajectory of ill health and male mortality bodes ill for the nation's ability to resolve its economic troubles (given an increasingly graying population) and creates concerns about its continued capacity to maintain a fighting force even at current levels of effectiveness.

Finally, the fact that economic, political, and demographic declines affect parts of Russia very differently, combined with increased regional political autonomy over the course of Russian independence and continuing concerns about interethnic and interregional tension, creates a danger that locality and/or ethnicity could become rallying cries for internal conflict.

While some might argue that Russia's weakness, or even the potential for its eventual collapse, has little to do with the United States, the truth is that a range of U.S. interests is directly affected by Russia's deterioration and the threats that it embodies. The dangers of proliferation or use of nuclear or other weapons of mass destruction (WMD), heightened by Russian weakness, quite directly threaten the United States and its vital interests. Organized crime in Russia is linked to a large and growing multinational network of criminal groups that threaten the United States and its economy both directly and through links with (and support of) global and local terrorist organizations. Russia is also a major energy producer and a transit state for oil and gas from the Caspian at a time when the U.S. government has identified that region, and energy interests in general, as key to its national security. Washington's allies, closer to Russia physically, are not only the customers for much of this energy but are also the likely victims of any refugee flows, environmental crises, or potential flare-ups of violence that Russian decline may spur. Finally, recent history suggests a strong possibility that the United States would play a role in seeking to alleviate a humanitarian crisis on or near Russian soil, whether it was caused by epidemic, war, or a nuclear/industrial catastrophe.

For the U.S. Air Force, this should be food for thought. Whatever operations the United States undertakes on or near the Russian landmass, the U.S. Air Force is certain to be heavily relied upon for transportation. In addition, a wide range of disparate military missions in a treacherous environment is foreseeable. The very factors that would make involvement more likely—uncertain central control, danger of WMD use or spread, epidemics, crime and corruption—will also make any military operations far more complicated and difficult.

These problems are intensified by an almost complete lack of planning on the U.S. military's part for such contingencies. U.S. military thinking about Russia has been largely limited to engagement activities, and operational efforts have been concentrated far more on the post-Soviet states on its periphery, a situation that has exacerbated U.S.-Russian tension. This situation is a result of both strategic and bureaucratic factors, and has as much to do with Russian attitudes as with the United States. However, combined with the dangerous tendencies in Russia, U.S. military lack of planning increases the likelihood that sometime in the next 15 years the United States could find itself operating almost blind, going into a theater without knowing the status of airfields, the loyalties and proclivities of those on the ground, or the difficult terrain itself.

The current recognition by both the United States and Russia of common ground in the security arena, and, indeed, of the need for cooperation in advancing shared goals in combating terrorism and WMD proliferation (despite differences in many of the specifics of how these problems are viewed), provides an important opportunity for changes in how the United States relates to the Russian Federation. To prepare for a wide range of possible future contingencies, increased cooperation and planning not only must be pursued for the direct benefits they will bring, but also must be combined with comprehensive thinking about the new challenges that a still-evolving Russia poses.

ACKNOWLEDGMENTS

The authors would like to thank, first of all, our colleagues in the Project AIR FORCE project "New Challenges for the U.S. Air Force," especially David Shlapak, David Thaler, and Dan Fox, who assisted us in thinking through some of the operational implications of the issues examined. William O'Malley's assistance in research and on the ground in Germany and Russia was also invaluable. Without the support and encouragement of Zalmay Khalilzad, former Director of Project AIR FORCE's Strategy and Doctrine Program, under whose auspices this study was initiated, and his successor, Edward Harshberger, none of this work would ever have seen light, and we owe them both a debt of gratitude. Alan Vick's support, assistance, and advice throughout the research and preparation of this report helped create a much-improved analysis. And, of course, none of this would have been possible without Lt Col Walter Diaz (USAF/XOPX), whose help and involvement greatly and repeatedly facilitated our research.

We are also extremely grateful to the many U.S. military and civilian personnel in Washington, Europe, and Moscow who assisted us as we carried out this study. While the sheer number of those who gave of their time and knowledge precludes naming them all, we would like to single out Lt Col Thomas Y. Headen and Maj Scott Herrick at USAFE (XPXS), COL Alan G. Stohlberg and LTC Frank Morgese at EUCOM (J-5), Gail Nelson of the Joint Analysis Center, Lt Col Dennis Larm and Capt Jonathan Laahs at the U.S. Embassy in Moscow, and Col Robert Boudreau and his staff at J-5 in the Pentagon.

In Moscow, we particularly thank Dmitri Trenin at the Carnegie Institute; Dmitry Kovchegin, Dmitry Polikanov, and Ivan Safranchuk at the PIR Center; Mikhail Moroshnichenko at GosAtomNadzor; Anatoliy Diakov, Timur Kadyshev, Eugene Miasnikov, and Pavel Podvig at the Center for Arms Control, Energy and Environmental Studies at the Moscow Institute for Physics and Technology; Emil Payin; and Leokadia Drobizheva.

Early drafts of this work benefited from the comments of John van Oudenaren, Thomas Graham, and Fritz Ermarth. Edward Warner's and Jeremy Azrael's numerous helpful suggestions greatly enhanced the quality of the report. Robert Nurick and D. J. Peterson provided tremendously useful assistance and advice. We are especially grateful to Joanna Alberdeston for her efforts in preparing this manuscript, which was no easy task, and to Jeanne Heller, our editor, whose efforts greatly enhanced its readability and flow.

With gratitude to all of the above and more, the authors point out that no one here listed is in any way responsible for any errors or oversights in this study; those, along with the views expressed here, are ours alone.

Chapter One

INTRODUCTION: STRATEGIC IMPLICATIONS OF RUSSIA'S DECLINE

Throughout most of the Cold War era, U.S. and NATO military planners prepared and trained to fight a massive land war in Europe (and elsewhere) against the Soviet Union and its allies, with the specter of nuclear exchange ever present in the background. In testament to the skills and capabilities of those planners and to U.S. and NATO military forces as a whole, this preparation and planning successfully deterred conflict and maintained an uneasy peace until the collapse of the USSR brought the Cold War to its end.

Today, Russia poses new threats to the United States and its allies. These are not the traditional threats rooted in an adversary's military capabilities but rather the somewhat more amorphous dangers presented by military, political, and social decline in a strategically important state. They affect U.S. interests directly and indirectly, and even suggest the possibility that one day U.S. military forces will be called for service in or near the Russian Federation itself. Now, as then, U.S. and allied planning and preparation could mitigate that threat as well as guarantee the capability to respond effectively and quickly.

In this report, we discuss the form, extent, and implications of Russia's deterioration and identify its effects on U.S. interests generally and those of the U.S. Air Force in particular. We also consider what actions can be taken now to prevent (or limit) this decline from becoming a threat to U.S. interests.

DECLINING, FAILING, AND DYSFUNCTIONAL STATES

To argue that Russia is a failed state is premature at best, misleading at worst. To argue that Russia is a fully functional entity, however, is also not entirely accurate. Today's Russia has declined from the pinnacles of capability, status, and power attributed (rightly or wrongly) to the Soviet Union at its height to a level low enough to have serious implications. That said, Russia remains a state of real power and influence, although with enormous internal and external problems.

It is often argued that declining or failing states increase the risk of international conflict,[1] particularly in the case of states that are, have been, or hope to become great powers. The mechanisms by which decline translates into war are several. One is that a state that sees itself as declining in power relative to others may seek to wage pre-emptive war, to fight while it can still win in hopes of retaining control of assets and power. Joseph Nye raises several historical examples of this phenomenon: Thucydides wrote that the Peloponnesian War was precipitated by a declining Sparta's fear of Athens' rise. Hundreds of years later, German fear of growing Russian strength led officials in Berlin to advocate war in 1914 rather than wait until the Russians grew even stronger. Britain entered that same conflict because it hoped to halt German growth, having been unable to reach accommodation with Germany as it had with other powers.[2]

Increasing domestic political disorder and chaos is another factor that can render a state more war-prone. It has been argued convincingly that political transition generally, whether to a democratic or an autocratic regime, is inherently unstable and increases the likelihood of war. In a democratizing state, the rise of groups and individuals who compete for power in part by appealing to ethnic or nationalist symbols and allegiances can promote conflict. If these symbols apply to only a portion of the population, antagonisms between

---

[1]Thomas Graham and Arnold Horelick, *U.S.-Russian Relations at the Turn of the Century*, Report of the U.S. Working Group on U.S.-Russian Relations, Carnegie Endowment for International Peace, Washington, DC, May 2000.

[2]Joseph S. Nye, Jr., *Bound to Lead: The Changing Nature of American Power*, Basic Books, New York, 1990. For more on how the decline of great powers can result in conflict, see A.F.K. Organski, *World Politics*, 2nd ed., Knopf, New York, 1968; and Robert Gilpin, *War and Change in World Politics*, Cambridge University Press, New York, 1981.

groups within and outside the state are created or exacerbated.[3] Internal political dissent, whether or not ethnically based, may also lead a state to seek war as a means of fostering unity against a common foe and thus overcoming internal strife.[4] In Russia's case, aspects of the 1999 invasion of the renegade province of Chechnya may fit such a pattern.

Finally, a declining state's weakness may invite attack from other states who see a window of opportunity to increase their own power through victory and/or conquest.[5] Geoffrey Blainey points out that wars are fought because combatants believe they can win. The decline of an adversary may well foster such a belief, while the declining state may not realize the extent of its weakness and fail to capitulate.[6] A variety of factors of regime transition—revolution, for instance—can lead outsiders to see a state as weak and vulnerable (rightly or wrongly).[7] Decline and state failure are less ambiguous in telegraphing weakness than is regime transition, and therefore might be considered even more likely to spur aggression on the part of others. If the states involved are great powers, their actions tend to have a significant impact throughout the international system, and the dangers of spreading conflict are similarly increased.[8]

If the general fact of Russia's decline raises concern, the specifics of it are no less important. Although Russia cannot be described as a "failed" or "failing" state, it does exhibit several attributes that have been associated with the processes of state failure. Insofar as these

---

[3]Edward D. Mansfield and Jack Snyder, "Democratization and the Danger of War," *International Security*, Vol. 20, No. 1, Summer 1995, pp. 5–38. While Mansfield and Snyder demonstrate that transitions as a whole are unstable, they find the fact that this pertains also to transitions to democracy particularly interesting, hence the title of their piece.

[4]See Geoffrey Blainey, *The Causes of War*, The Free Press, 1988 edition, New York, pp. 72–86.

[5]For an argument on how and why conquest continues to be advantageous to the conqueror, see Peter Liberman, "The Spoils of Conquest," *International Security*, Vol. 18, No. 2, Fall 1993, pp. 125–153.

[6]See discussion in Blainey, *The Causes of War*, pp. 72–86, 123.

[7]Stephen M. Walt, *Revolution and War*, Cornell University Press, Ithaca and London, 1996, p. 32.

[8]On the rise and decline of great powers and resulting proclivities to conflict, see Organski, *World Politics*; and Gilpin, *War and Change in World Politics*.

processes, and not merely the fact of failure itself, make a state a danger to its own people and the international community, it is worth considering the relevant literature as it applies to Russia.

A state might be thought to be headed toward failure when there are significant concerns about its ability to function as a cohesive and effective centrally governed entity. Civil war and political disintegration may be the results of state failure, but some key indicators that the processes are under way include:

- The absence of a functioning economic system;

- The emergence of rampant corruption and a criminal economy (that takes the place of the absent legal economy);

- The emergence of privatized institutions for personal security; and

- The disintegration of military morale, capability, and command and control.[9]

In short, a state fails when basic rationales for why people come together under a central government—guaranteed personal security, enforcement of the rules of economic transactions, and a reasonable sense of protection from external threat—cease to be effectively served by existing institutions.

While these factors all serve as indicators that a state is declining in particularly dangerous ways, their presence does not necessarily indicate that the state has already failed or even that it will fail in the future. While we can recognize a completely failed state—central control is absent, law and order is nonexistent, and militaries, if they exist, are privatized—there is no clear understanding of what point along the path to decline marks irreversibility, or the greatest danger. It is, however, clear that these indicators serve not only as signposts

---

[9]It should be noted that state failure is not synonymous with territorial disintegration. On state failure see, Steven R. David, "Saving America from the Coming Civil Wars," *Foreign Affairs*, Vol. 78, No. 1, Winter 1999, pp. 103–116; Gerald Helman and Steven R. Ratner, "Saving Failed States," *Foreign Policy*, No. 89, Winter 1992–1993, pp. 3–20; David Hoffman, "Yeltsin's Absentee Rule Raises the Specter of a 'Failed State,'" *Washington Post*, February 26, 1999, p. A1.

of possible state failure but also as dangerous developments in their own right.

Because the dangers posed by a state's decline are often not limited by the borders of that state, outside actors may seek to take steps to halt or reverse the decline (even as, as noted above, others may try to take advantage of it). In addition to the increased risk of conflict, other effects of state deterioration can worry neighbors and others. Internal or international conflict can create refugee problems for nearby states, straining resources and potentially exporting political instability. In today's interdependent world, an increasingly criminalized economy in one state contributes to the rise of criminal activity globally. Thus, when a failing or weak state is unable to respond to crises that affect other states' security interests, its neighbors or other parties may take matters into their own hands.

IS RUSSIA IN DECLINE?

To what extent are the processes of decline and the dangers they embody present in Russia? In this report, we argue that there exist real concerns about the direction of trends in political and economic development, the health and well-being of the population, the state of the Russian military, and the condition of Russia's nuclear power plants and its nuclear-related sector. Moreover, the regional variation in these problems creates additional concerns about the potential for internal unrest and division.

We focus on a few key areas in which recent trends suggest significant decline. These areas do not comprise the sum total of Russia's problems, but we believe they do include the problems that are most likely to lead to crises that affect U.S. interests and might escalate to involve U.S. forces.

First, the continuing evolution of Russia's political and economic structures and institutions is moving in some potentially disturbing directions. It is unclear as yet to what extent President Vladimir Putin and his administration will be able to reverse the processes of political decentralization that gathered force during his predecessor's tenure. Although the current administration has taken a number of steps to reassert central control, the divergence in regional economic, political, and demographic indicators suggests that administrative changes may be insufficient to stem this trend and that efforts to do so may even backfire. Moreover, the costs to public and press freedoms that Putin's other reforms appear to be engendering create additional concerns for Russia's future.

The prevalence of corruption and the "routinization" of crime or force in economic life are further symptoms of decline, as is the trend toward the demonetization of Russia's economy. Although recent indicators of economic growth in Russia are positive, their basis in high oil prices and a weak ruble suggests that without comprehensive reform they are likely not sustainable.

Russia's shrinking population suffers from low fertility as well as from high rates of disease and shockingly high levels of mortality among working-age males. If these trends continue, Russia will face a continued graying of its population, which will place added strain on its economy. It will also raise concerns about Russia's ability to man its military. Finally, insofar as demographic factors, no less than economic and political factors, affect regions and ethnic groups differently, they have the potential to play into efforts to mobilize parts of the population in ways that increase the risk of interethnic or interregional conflict, although this is not highly likely.

The Russian military is affected not only by the problems of the country as a whole but by difficulties of its own. The demographic downtrends mean that each year the young men who report for duty are sicker and fewer. The collapse of law and order means that many have criminal backgrounds. The existing military structures are not immune, and tales of corruption and crime extend to the highest levels. Underfunding and poor maintenance continue to take their toll. Equipment ages unrepaired, and troops are sent into battle without adequate training. Soldiers and officers go without pay for months at a time and are increasingly dependent on local governments for political, financial, and other support. In this environment, order and discipline must be questioned, with potentially terrifying implications especially for Russia's nuclear weapons arsenal and related infrastructure, although the impact on the conventional forces alone is sufficient grounds for serious concern.

Finally, there is the decline in Russia's transportation and industrial sectors, including the civilian nuclear power sector. There are mixed reports about the state of Russia's road, rail, and other transport networks. Although the networks appear to be functioning, they are far from a peak condition of efficiency and safety. In the industrial sectors, including nuclear power, production and efficiency are low, workers are unpaid for months at a time, and facilities are aging. The risk of accidents and the difficulties of responding to such accidents quickly and effectively are thus increased.

These factors, singly and together, increase the likelihood of crisis and demonstrate the extent of Russia's decline as a great power. While Russia's relative weakness makes it unlikely that it will wage aggressive war against another great power, the theory and experience of both declining states and those undergoing complex and uncertain transitions suggest the possibility of Russia lashing out against a neighbor or a weaker state. The possibility of internal conflict rooted in ethnic tension within Russia or its political devolution is also increased.

Both increased conflict propensity and Russian infrastructure deterioration in turn increase the likelihood of a humanitarian catastrophe, whether from war itself, from an industrial or nuclear accident, from a health crisis, or from physical and economic isolation of parts of the country. Whether the result is refugees; hunger and mass starvation; spread of radiation; or an epidemic, the situation is unlikely to be limited to Russian soil alone. Moreover, Russian weakness makes it more difficult for its own security and emergency forces to effectively respond, aggravating the problem. There are those who would argue that while this bodes ill for Russia, it has little impact on the United States. Such an argument ignores several key U.S. interests that are directly affected by Russia's future.

- **The security of Washington's European and Asian allies who are directly affected by what happens in and near Russia and by stability on Russia's periphery**. Whether the threat is from radiation or refugees or involves the spread of violence, U.S. allies have excellent reasons to fear an increased Russian propensity to crisis.

- **The secure and reliable export of energy resources from the Caspian basin.**[10] Most of the export pipelines from the Caspian basin go through Russia. Furthermore, Russia's strong interests in the Caspian ensure that it will remain deeply involved there, even if more non-Russian pipelines are built.

- **The assurance of nuclear security and prevention of nuclear use, either sanctioned or otherwise.** Insofar as Russian deterioration increases the risks that portions of its nuclear weapons stockpile (or other materials) could be employed or diverted into dangerous hands, the United States has a vital interest in these events.

- **The prevention of the rise, growth, maintenance, or acquisition of weapons of mass destruction (WMD) by terrorist groups.** The growth of criminal activity in Russia combined with the potential for failure of central control in parts of the country create a real danger of cooperation between criminals and terrorist groups in ways that can hurt the United States and/or its allies. The threat of diversion or acquisition of nuclear or other WMD material by either criminal or terrorist groups also cannot be ignored.

- **The alleviation of mass human suffering wherever it may occur.** The United States has set precedents of willingness and ability to help when a wide range of states have faced humanitarian catastrophes. Washington could well feel a similar imperative to assist Russia in a crisis situation.[11]

In succeeding chapters, we discuss these key factors of Russia's decline and how continuing deterioration could lead to crisis in ways that affect U.S. interests. We then present a set of notional scenarios for how events could unfold such that the United States might face

---

[10]U.S. officials have repeatedly described Caspian energy resources as a key strategic interest, some even going so far as to call it a vital interest (see, for example, Federico Peña, then U.S. Secretary of Energy, in his testimony on the "U.S. Role in the Caucasus and Central Asia," before the House International Relations Committee on April 30, 1998).

[11]Operation Provide Hope airlifted food supplies to Russia and other post-Soviet states when the Soviet collapse hampered food and medical distribution throughout the area. Other historical cases of U.S. assistance to various Russian governments include the sending of troops to the Far East in 1918 to guard the railways and assistance under Lend-Lease during World War II.

an imperative to respond with military forces and assets. Finally, we consider the implications for U.S. planning and lay out some recommendations for the future.

Chapter Two

REGIONAL AUTONOMY OR INCREASED CENTRALIZATION?

TRENDS TOWARD POLITICAL AND ECONOMIC DECENTRALIZATION

For over 70 years, the political infrastructure of the Soviet Union was cemented by the Communist Party's nearly complete monopoly over state power and control. The party could reward loyalty and obedience to its ideology and punish those who failed to follow its orders. Top administrative posts were conferred on reliable party leaders and policy planning took place almost exclusively in Moscow. Although local authorities had some autonomy in how they divided up rewards and implemented directives from Moscow, the Soviet Union was truly a top-down state, quite different from federal models such as that of the United States, where the federal components enjoy significant policy autonomy. Soviet officials (and others) argued that such strict control was necessitated by the size of the Soviet Union and the nature of its centrally planned economy.[1]

---

[1]For an excellent discussion of how Moscow controlled the regions into the Khrushchev period, see Merle Fainsod, *How Russia Is Ruled*, Harvard University Press, Cambridge, Massachusetts, 1963. On transitions under way by 1980 see Jerry Hough, *Soviet Leadership in Transition*, The Brookings Institution, Washington, DC, 1980. For the Gorbachev years, an excellent source is Jerry Hough, *Russia and the West: Gorbachev and the Politics of Reform*, Simon and Schuster, New York, 1990. On the early days of transition, see Geoffrey Hosking, *The Awakening of the Soviet Union*, Harvard University Press, Cambridge, Massachusetts, 1991.

This centralized model of Soviet governance began to loosen when Gorbachev came to power and began implementing a series of policies generally referred to as *perestroika*. During this period, the Communist Party's monopoly over economic planning was relaxed and some limited free enterprise was permitted. The process was of course hastened and completed by (and, some may argue, helped cause) the collapse of the USSR—and with it the Soviet political and economic system—a few years later. But the transition from Soviet rule and economic planning to democracy and a free market that many envisioned at the time has proven a very bumpy road, and Russia's particular path on it remains far from certain. Political and economic reform capable of spanning Russia's vast territory and overcoming the legacies of the Soviet past has proven difficult to define or effect. The Russian economy and polity today can be seen as a combination of Soviet institutions, Western models, anarchy, and some strange mutations of each of the three.

One component of this is governance itself, both in large cities like Moscow and St. Petersburg and in the far-off regions. Many of Russia's current leaders—including President Vladimir Putin—were successful administrators and government functionaries in Soviet times and are products of that system. The extent to which they have adapted to new approaches rather than adapting the new Russia to their own attitudes and relationships is a matter for debate.

Through the late 1990s, an increasing perception in Moscow and the regions (as well as on the part of some Western scholars) was that Russia was on the verge of disintegrating into its component parts, that as regional officials realized that they were largely on their own, their economies and policies grew more and more isolated from Moscow. Indeed, some regions, most notably those deemed by the Soviets to be "homelands" of specific ethnic groups, clearly sought more political autonomy. Tatarstan for a time refused to pay federal taxes or send its young men to serve in Russia's army, declared its "sovereignty," negotiated an agreement governing its relations with Russia, and appointed trade representatives separate from Moscow's in 14 locations outside of Russia. Variations on this theme were also played out by Chechnya, Bashkiria, and Yakutia. Independent "foreign policies" were also taken on by non-ethnic regions. The governor of Primorsky Krai was able to delay the implementation of a 1991 border agreement with China for eight years (until 1999). The governor of Sverdlovsk appointed a minister of economic and foreign relations for his region. In fact, over the course of the 1990s, Russia's regional governments signed over 1000 agreements with partners in dozens of countries and many sent official representatives abroad, although the success of these efforts was questionable.[2]

Moreover, many regional laws and local constitutions were in direct contradiction to the Russian constitution and federal law. Examples include a 1998 Tatarstan citizenship law that permitted Tatar citizenship without Russian citizenship and the legislation of Bashkortostan, which at the end of 2001 included some 184 laws and 179 decrees of the Bashkortostan Cabinet of Ministers (about 72 percent of the region's legislation) that were in contravention of federal law.[3] Another illustrative case is the effort by Krasnoyarsk's colorful late governor, General Aleksandr Lebed', to market his region's capacity for nuclear-waste processing to foreign customers—in flagrant contravention of federal law against the processing of foreign nuclear waste.

Regional offices and branches of federal agencies, although formally reporting to Moscow, grew increasingly linked to local governments, receiving funding from their budgets and in many cases requiring a local governor's approval for federal appointments to the region.[4] A similar pattern emerged with military forces stationed throughout the country and with industry, particularly the nuclear sector (discussed in greater detail below).

---

[2]"Bashkortostan's Violations of Federal Laws Tallied," *RFE/RL Newsline*, Vol. 5, No. 242, Part I, December 28, 2001; Graeme P. Herd, "Russia: Systemic Transformation or Federal Collapse?" *Journal of Peace Research*, Vol. 36, No. 3, 1999; Emil A. Payin, "Ethnic Separatism," in Jeremy R. Azrael and Emil A. Payin (eds.), *Conflict and Consensus in Ethno-Political and Center-Periphery Relations in Russia*, RAND, CF-139, 1998, p. 17; Mikhail Alexseev, "Russia's Periphery in the Global Arena: Do Regions Matter in the Kremlin's Foreign Policy?" Washington, DC, Program on New Approaches to Russian Security (PONARS), Center for Strategic and International Studies, 2000.

[3]"Bashkortostan's Violations of Federal Laws Tallied"; Herd, "Russia: Systemic Transformation or Federal Collapse?" Payin, "Ethnic Separatism"; Alexseev, "Russia's Periphery in the Global Arena: Do Regions Matter in the Kremlin's Foreign Policy?"

[4]Alexseev, "Russia's Periphery in the Global Arena: Do Regions Matter in the Kremlin's Foreign Policy?" Daniel S. Treisman, *After the Deluge: Regional Crises and Political Consolidation in Russia*, The University of Michigan Press, Ann Arbor, Michigan, 2001, pp. 12–14.

On the economic level, the regions became increasingly isolated from one another throughout the 1990s. Treisman traces this to the inefficiency of the Soviet supply chains that had linked these economies in the past. With the Soviet structures gone, the costs of interregional business and transport grew, and it became less advantageous to trade with other regions.[5] After the economic collapse of August 1998, a number of regions including Krasnoyarsk, Kemerovo, Tatarstan, Altay, and Volgograd took steps to codify protectionist policies, passing laws that prevented the export of food or other commodities outside the region and hoarding products within their own regions.[6]

Economic regionalization has gone hand in hand with a deepening of inequalities among the regions. Vladimir Popov argues that rich regions—those with resource wealth—have been far more successful in the transition than poorer regions. They also enjoy a better quality of life overall, with less crime despite higher levels of labor mobility and continuing income inequalities. Ten regions accounted for 60 percent of Russia's foreign trade in 1998, and the majority of that trade was concentrated around Moscow and Tyumen. Moreover, 81 percent of foreign direct investment in Russia in 1997 went to Moscow, Tatarstan, Omsk, or Krasnoyarsk. Although the Russian government has been consistent in redistributing income through subsidies and similar mechanisms from wealthier to poorer regions, this disparity continues to grow.[7]

Scholars who observed this process developed a range of arguments as to its implications and causes. Some saw it as indicative of state breakdown and decay.[8] Richard Ericson writes that it represented a

---

[5]George Breslauer et al., "Russia at the End of Yel'tsin's Presidency," *Post-Soviet Affairs,* Vol. 16, No. 1, 2000; Treisman, *After the Deluge: Regional Crises and Political Consolidation in Russia.*

[6]Clifford G. Gaddy and Barry William Ickes, *Stability and Disorder: An Evolutionary Analysis of Russia's Virtual Economy,* The Davidson Institute, 1999; Herd, "Russia: Systemic Transformation or Federal Collapse?"

[7]Alexseev, "Russia's Periphery in the Global Arena: Do Regions Matter in the Kremlin's Foreign Policy?" Vladimir Popov, "Reform Strategies and Economic Performance of Russia's Regions," *World Development,* Vol. 29, No. 5, 2001.

[8]Alexseev cites Herd, "Russia: Systemic Transformation or Federal Collapse?" D. V. Olshansky, *Alternative Scenarios of the Disintegration of the Russian Federation,*

new Russian economic structure: "industrial feudalism." Russia, he argues, is feudal in its hierarchical structure of small nobility, laboring masses, and weak and small middle class as well as its decentralization and conflation of political, economic, and social roles. Other feudal aspects include the personalization of authority and discretion and semi-autarchic socioeconomic units, in the form of enterprises and associations. The regions are able to manage their own economies along political preferences and restrict imports and exports. The central government provides financial support directly and indirectly through subsidies and negotiated taxes. The system is furthered by local renationalization of property through bankruptcy procedures and tax offsets and demonetization plays a role in supporting the development of local scrip. All of this, Ericson writes, has led to the devolution of responsibilities to regional elites who control social services and funds.[9]

Another perspective was to see the increased political and economic regionalization as a result of political bargaining on the part of then President Yeltsin, who traded regional autonomy for support from local leaders for his weak rule, being easily threatened by dissent and unrest into buying off opposition and separatist forces with resources from the center.[10] Others argued, however, that the system that emerged during the Yeltsin years was carefully calibrated give and take, with regions signaling the center of their needs and dissatisfaction through dissent, unrest, and independent-minded behavior, and being rewarded with economic (subsidies, tax breaks) and political benefits that kept them (again with the exception of Chechnya) within the Russian fold and avoided conflict.[11] Treisman, for instance, provides evidence that financial transfers from the center to specific regions rose as dissent in those regions rose, and Popov notes that direct financial transfers tended to go to those re-

---

Potomac Foundation, McLean, Virginia, 1993; Jean Radovanyi, "And What If Russia Breaks Up?" *Post-Soviet Geography*, Vol. 33, June 1992, as providing this view.

[9]Breslauer et al., "Russia at the End of Yel'tsin's Presidency."

[10]Matthew Evangelista, "Russia's Path to a New Regional Policy," PONARS, 2000.

[11]Mikhail Alexseev, "Decentralization Versus State Collapse: Explaining Russia's Endurance," *Journal of Peace Research*, Vol. 38, No. 1, January 2001; Herd, "Russia: Systemic Transformation or Federal Collapse"; Treisman, *After the Deluge: Regional Crises and Political Consolidation in Russia.*

gions that lobbied the most and had the most ability to upset the federal government.[12]

Alexseev argues that not only was this the case in the Yeltsin years, but this form of "asymmetric federalism" is a necessity for Russia's continued survival. By providing checks and balances between the center and the periphery, he writes, this system gives the regions incentive to remain within Russia and to work with the federal government. Without such a system of selective incentives, the regions will see advantages in uniting against the Kremlin, linking civic and ethnic grievances that the Yeltsin system kept under wraps. Moreover, the loss of their benefits will increase their sense of grievance against the center.[13]

GOVERNMENT RESPONSE

By the end of the 1990s, there was increasing fear that the center was losing its capacity to govern, and that the regions were increasingly governing themselves independently of Moscow. Graeme P. Herd dates this to the August 1998 economic collapse and cites then Prime Minister Primakov's statement that "we are facing a very serious threat of our country being split up."[14] Mikhail Alexseev argues that Russia's perception of internal weakness, and "vulnerability to regional disintegration, economic contraction, and demographic decline" combined with the strength of other states and groups, created a security dilemma for Russia that was reflected in its foreign policy.[15]

Efforts to stem this perceived disintegration have taken many forms. A law passed by the Duma in 1999 required regions to provide advance notice of upcoming negotiations with non-Russian entities and to submit drafts of any agreements to the Ministry of Foreign

---

[12]Popov, "Reform Strategies and Economic Performance of Russia's Regions"; Treisman, *After the Deluge: Regional Crises and Political Consolidation in Russia*.

[13]Alexseev, "Decentralization Versus State Collapse: Explaining Russia's Endurance"; Mikhail Alexseev, "The Unintended Consequences of Anti-Federalist Centralization in Russia," PONARS, 2000.

[14]Herd, "Russia: Systemic Transformation or Federal Collapse?"

[15]Alexseev, "Russia's Periphery in the Global Arena: Do Regions Matter in the Kremlin's Foreign Policy?"

Affairs, and to register and make public those agreements.[16] Other proposals considered by the federal government during the early months of the Putin administration included imposing more stringent controls over federal funds spent throughout the country, canceling gubernatorial (presidential in ethnic autonomous regions) elections, imposing direct rule from Moscow, and limiting the financing of the courts to the federal government.[17]

In the end, Putin implemented several policies geared at least in part to increasing central control. One of his first steps was to create a new system of governance, overlaying seven administrative districts on top of his country's 89 existing regions. These districts coincide more with Russia's military districts than with regional borders. This had the immediate effect of reducing the number of presidential representatives to the regions from Yeltsin's 89 to Putin's seven. However, where Yeltsin's representatives proved increasingly dependent on local leaders, most of Putin's (five of the seven appointed) had a federal military or security background.[18] Those who did not—like Sergei Kiriyenko, assigned to oversee the central Volga region—have former KGB and security officials on their staff.[19]

Putin's representatives, or governors-general, were tasked with overseeing police, tax, and other federal officials in their districts and with bringing local laws in line with federal legislation.[20] Some revived the Soviet/Tsarist tradition of federal inspectors who can conduct audits of regional administrations.[21] The appointment of these representatives also created a new layer of bureaucracy between local officials and the Kremlin.[22] If in Yeltsin's time regional leaders would approach the president and his staff directly with their prob-

---

[16]Ibid.

[17]Alexseev, "The Unintended Consequences of Anti-Federalist Centralization in Russia."

[18]Steve Solnik, "The New Federal Structure: More Centralized or More of the Same?" PONARS, 2000.

[19]Evangelista, "Russia's Path to a New Regional Policy."

[20]Martin Nicholson, "Putin's Russia: Slowing the Pendulum Without Stopping the Clock," *International Affairs,* Vol. 77, No. 3, 2001.

[21]Solnik, "The New Federal Structure: More Centralized or More of the Same?"

[22]Evangelista, "Russia's Path to a New Regional Policy"; Solnik, "The New Federal Structure: More Centralized or More of the Same?"

lems and concerns, they were now directed to address them to the governors-general.

Another change implemented by Putin was to fundamentally re-structure the Federation Council, a legislative body somewhat comparable to the U.S. Senate and composed of the governors/presidents and parliamentary speakers of Russia's 89 regions. Initially, Putin planned to eliminate the council altogether. Over time, however, the plan evolved to a restructuring of the Federal Council. Whereas before its membership was composed of the regional executive and legislative leadership, it is now made up by their (full-time) representatives. One representative is elected from each region by the regional parliament and one is appointed by the governor/president with terms running as long as those who appointed them (the speaker of the parliament or the governor/president) remain in office.[23]

A third move was the creation of a judicial process to remove regional leaders on grounds of violation of the federal constitution. There are two components to this reform. The first gives the president leverage over local leaders. The second provides a mechanism for bringing local law into compliance with federal law.[24] Other aspects of legal reform include legislation developed by the Duma by mid-2001 (but which will not be implemented until 2003 at the earliest) that is geared to increasing funding for courts (to include pay for judges), better oversight, and increased concern for the rights of prisoners and the accused (extending trial by jury beyond the nine Russian regions where it now exists, limiting time on remand, etc.). This legislation would also impose sanctions for regional violation of Constitutional Court rulings. The legislation is opposed by Russia's procurator general and his office, whose powers would be significantly limited if these laws take effect.[25]

---

[23]Solnik, "The New Federal Structure: More Centralized or More of the Same"; Natalia Yefimova, "New Faces but Old Loyalties in Senate," *Johnson's Russia List (Moscow Times)*, January 15, 2002.

[24]Nicholson, "Putin's Russia: Slowing the Pendulum Without Stopping the Clock"; Solnik, "The New Federal Structure: More Centralized or More of the Same?"

[25]Nicholson, "Putin's Russia: Slowing the Pendulum Without Stopping the Clock."

Putin also sought to take steps to curtail regional efforts to conduct independent foreign trade and eliminate special tax status (some regions were exempt from federal tax), as well as making more fundamental changes to the tax code as a whole with reform of value-added taxes (VAT) and other taxes to centralize the flow of revenues and removal of the provisions that enabled a 50-50 split of tax revenues with regional governments.[26]   Finally, the Kremlin openly sponsored candidates in regional elections and pressured current regional leaders to step down at the end of their terms of office.   In fact, Nikolai Petrov asserts that incumbents were threatened with prosecution on various charges if they ran for reelection, and they were offered seats on the new Federation Council if they agreed not to run.[27]

The effectiveness of these policies has been mixed.   While there is a great deal of variation in how the governors-general have interpreted their roles and it does not appear that any of them have been coopted by the regional governments to date, at least some of them reportedly have had difficulty asserting control, sometimes finding themselves ignored by local officials.[28]   The postponement by the federal treasury of its planned reorganization along district lines maintains a system of branches in all 89 regions, limiting the ability of governors-general to control the flow of federal funding to the individual regions.   Vladimir Gel'man argues that although the presidential envoys try to influence regional affairs, they lack the "tools" (direct control over property rights, investment programs) to do so.   Moreover, because local branches of federal agencies are subordinate to the ministries in Moscow, not to the governors-general, the latter have little ability to affect their behavior.[29]

---

[26]Evangelista, "Russia's Path to a New Regional Policy"; Vladimir Gel'man, "The Rise and Fall of Federal Reform in Russia," PONARS, 2001.

[27]Aleksey Makarkin, "The regions try on epaulets" (in Russian), *Segodnya*, August 1, 2000, Internet edition, www.segodnya.ru/w3s.nsf/Contents/2000_167_polit_text_makarkin1.html; Nikolai Petrov, "Policization Versus Democratization," PONARS, 2001.

[28]Peter Baker and Susan B. Glasser, "Regions Resist Kremlin Control," *Washington Post*, May 31, 2001; Nicholson, "Putin's Russia: Slowing the Pendulum Without Stopping the Clock."

[29]Gel'man, "The Rise and Fall of Federal Reform in Russia."

Although Sergei Kiriyenko in the Volga region reported in May 2001 that he had replaced over half of the region's prosecutors who were failing to enforce federal law and was overseeing the rewriting of hundreds of laws,[30] hundreds of laws throughout Russia remain noncompliant with federal legislation and the Russian constitution.[31] The process to remove regional leaders on the basis of violation of the federal constitution is lengthy and involves the courts and the Duma, as well as warning periods, reviews, and so forth.[32]

The Kremlin was able to convince a number of local governors to step down or not run for reelection, but only at a cost of various side deals (for example, the Far East's Nazdratenko resigned but was given the post of chair of the Federal Fisheries Committee).[33] Kremlin-backed candidates in local elections had mixed results, losing, for example, in the important regions of Primorsky Krai and Nizhny Novgorod.[34] Putin eventually agreed to allow several local officials to run for a third term (rather than impose a two-term limit) and increased the power of the regions relative to that of cities and towns.[35]

The new Federation Council held its first meeting in January 2002. The individuals who have taken their seats reflect the mixed results of Putin's reform efforts. Natalia Yefimova writes that "most of the 146 senators approved . . . fit into one or more of several overlapping groups: regional leaders, big business, Kremlin protégés or former Cabinet officials and 'honorary retirees,' such as the handful of governors who gave up their gubernatorial posts to clear the way for more powerful—usually Moscow-backed—candidates." Many of them, particularly those who come from the business world, are Moscow-based and represent regions to which they have few per-

---

[30]Baker and Glasser, "Regions Resist Kremlin Control"; Nicholson, "Putin's Russia: Slowing the Pendulum Without Stopping the Clock."

[31]Gel'man, "The Rise and Fall of Federal Reform in Russia."

[32]Nicholson, "Putin's Russia: Slowing the Pendulum Without Stopping the Clock"; Solnik, "The New Federal Structure: More Centralized or More of the Same?"

[33]Baker and Glasser, "Regions Resist Kremlin Control"; Nicholson, "Putin's Russia: Slowing the Pendulum Without Stopping the Clock."

[34]Gel'man, "The Rise and Fall of Federal Reform in Russia."

[35]Nicholson, "Putin's Russia: Slowing the Pendulum Without Stopping the Clock."

sonal ties. Yefimova speculates that they might have made their own deals, perhaps promising financial or other assistance to poorer regions, to get their appointments.[36]

The Kremlin also tempered its tax reform efforts, with side deals to places like St. Petersburg and Tyumen to provide subsidies to make up for the losses in tax revenue that would result from turning more over to Moscow. That said, republics like Bashkortostan and Tatarstan, formerly exempt from paying taxes, complained about the new policies, but did pay (or agreed to pay) the necessary monies to the center.[37]

Much as Yeltsin's relations with the provinces were the subject of academic debate as to the intentions and mechanisms operating on both sides, several explanations have been advanced for the Putin administration's relationships with the regions. Steve Solnik argues that Putin has been successful in creating incentives for regional leaders to compete with each other to demonstrate support for the center.[38] Martin Nicholson suggests that regional leaders' willingness to go along with Putin now is a factor of their desire to stay in power and their fear that opposition will cost them that power. Their long-term loyalty, he writes, is therefore more questionable.[39]

In the economic realm, whether because of Putin's policies or for other reasons entirely, some of the processes of disintegration appear to be reversing. Nicholson writes that since 2000, the regional trend in business has been shifting to more cross-regional horizontal and vertical mergers, and financial-industrial groups with interests beyond a specific region are becoming more common.[40] Moreover, Yoshiko Herrera cites research by Daniel Berkowitz and David DeJong on regional commodity markets in Russia which suggests that the trends were in the direction of integration for 1994–1995,

---

[36]Gel'man, "The Rise and Fall of Federal Reform in Russia"; Yefimova, "New Faces but Old Loyalties in Senate."

[37]Evangelista, "Russia's Path to a New Regional Policy"; Steve Solnik, "Putin and the Provinces," PONARS, 2000.

[38]Solnik, "Putin and the Provinces."

[39]Nicholson, "Putin's Russia: Slowing the Pendulum Without Stopping the Clock."

[40]Ibid.

"disconnectedness" or regionalization in 1996–1997, and returned to integration in 1998–1999.[41]

The extent to which Putin can, or hopes to, impose central control over the regions is unknown. The status quo suggests a precarious stability, with a number of regional industrial, media, and other business interests remaining important,[42] while the overall trends lean toward a more centrally responsive Russia.

If Russia's bloody war in Chechnya seems unlikely to conclude in the immediate future, it is equally unlikely that more Chechnyas will emerge, in part because of the bloody example on the southern border and in part because of the very different ethnic, nationalist, and religious dynamics that operated in Chechnya compared to elsewhere in Russia.[43] The long-term challenge will involve finding the right blend of federalism and centralization—identifying the right trades and incentives—to keep Russia together and functional. Yeltsin's approach to the issue and Putin's appear to be very different, but both ended up negotiating with regional leaders to gain the level of control they felt was necessary.

While Alexseev is probably correct to argue that some level of federalism is required in a sustainable political system for Russia, a federalism that involves constant conflict between the regions and the center, as well as independent foreign policies on the part of some of the regions, is an inefficient use of resources at best and is potentially hazardous to Russia's future. Moreover, as this report will show, Russia's regions exhibit significant differentiation by economic and demographic indicators. This, combined with the developing alliances between regional governments and local military and industrial leadership and the fact that some of the regions are ethnically defined, means that regionalization presents yet another basket of dangers. As Mansfield and Snyder point out, one of the reasons that democratizing states are at particular risk of domestic conflict is that political entrepreneurs use ethnicity and other separatist ideals to

[41]Yoshiko M. Herrera, "Attempts Under Putin to Create a Unified Economic Space in Russia," PONARS, 2001.

[42]Solnik, "The New Federal Structure: More Centralized or More of the Same?"

[43]See Payin, "Ethnic Separatism."

motivate portions of the population, stirring up internecine hatred with the potential to lead to conflict between various groups.[44] The differences between the regions have the potential to feed into just such a cycle by creating regionally (and/or ethnically) based grievances and increasing self-identification with the region. Even if such an evolution does not lead to conflict, it could do grave damage to Russia's developing civil society.

---

[44]Mansfield and Snyder, "Democratization and the Danger of War."

Chapter Three

THE RUSSIAN ECONOMY

DEMONETIZATION, REFORM, AND POVERTY

Many useful accounts of the post–1991 evolution of the Russian economy provide an overview of the early days of privatization and the difficulties of reform throughout the 1990s.[1] Regionalization aside, the Russian economy remains in flux, with a variety of pathologies that have proven remarkably sustainable. Although recent indicators show significant improvement, it is unlikely that the economic turnaround will be sufficiently long-lasting to speedily complete the transformation to market economy that so many expected a decade ago.

Some blame reform efforts themselves for the continued problems facing the Russian economic system. Janine Wedel argues that the administration of foreign aid to Russia (and other post-Soviet states) may actually have discouraged privatization by helping specific groups and individuals gain power at the expense of reform efforts (and other groups and individuals). Moreover, she writes, the politically driven administration of foreign aid reinforced the dangerous

---

[1]See, for example, Anders Åslund, *How Russia Became a Market Economy*, The Brookings Institution, Washington, DC, 1995; Maxim Boycko, Andrei Shleifer, and Robert Vishny, *Privatizing Russia*, The MIT Press, Cambridge, Massachusetts, 1995; David Woodruff, *Money Unmade: Barter and the Fate of Russian Capitalism*, Cornell University Press, Ithaca and London, 1999.

interdependence of politics and economics that remains a key negative factor in the Russian economy today.[2]

Daniel Kotz blames the reasoning behind the reforms—the neo-liberal transition strategy. He argues that unlike in China, where the state socialist system remained in place while capitalism was allowed to develop gradually, the existing system was dismantled in Russia and firms were expected to privatize and function in an unplanned system with no support or backup.[3]

The effectiveness of reform efforts is, indeed, difficult to measure. Popov's research suggests that reforms, which are unevenly implemented from region to region, do not appear to lead to higher output per se but rather increase income concentration, shifting funds from worse-performing and poorer regions to wealthier and better-performing regions (somewhat overshadowed by government flows in the other direction, as discussed in the previous chapter). The result is a number of "safe liberal havens"—relatively prosperous low-crime regions with large shadow economies which have far greater income than other regions. Output and investment are apparently not significantly increased by the reforms themselves.[4]

It would make sense that the resource base remains the primary determinant of wealth in Russia if, as Josef Brada argues, Russia's comparative advantage exists only in energy and raw materials. Russian exports have not grown much (about 3 percent per year in the 1990s), especially when compared with East European economies that have seen significant export growth, but Russia has become increasingly dependent on its exports, particularly of energy. Brada notes that

---

[2]Janine R. Wedel, "U.S. Assistance for Market Reforms: Foreign Aid Failures in Russia and the Former Soviet Bloc," Cato Institute, Washington, DC, 1999. For more on errors and problems of Western assistance to Russia, a good overview is David Wedgewood Benn, "Review Article: Warm Words and Harsh Advice: A Critique of the West's Role in Russian Reforms," *International Affairs*, Vol. 77, No. 4, 2001, pp. 947–955. Benn reviews *The Tragedy of Russia's Reforms: Market Bolshevism Against Democracy* by Peter Reddaway and Dmitri Glinski; *Failed Crusade: America and the Tragedy of Post-Communist Russia* by Stephen F. Cohen; *The New Russia: Transition Gone Awry* by Lawrence R. Klein and Marshall Pomer (eds.).

[3]David M. Kotz, "Is Russia Becoming Capitalist?" *Science and Society,* Vol. 65, No. 2, Summer 2001.

[4]Popov, "Reform Strategies and Economic Performance of Russia's Regions."

Russia is the only transition state to sustain a large trade and current-account surplus throughout the 1990s. Its rates of capital flight (see below) have led to net resource outflows. Russian trade flows suggest a process of deindustrialization and increasing competitiveness in a structure that is likely to continue to inflict the brunt of the resulting pain on the average Russian.[5]

Another key factor of the Russian economy is a now seemingly slowed trend toward demonetization. Popov argues that this is in part a result of tight monetary policy in a system with weak institutions, which increases the likelihood of nonpayments and barter.[6] David Woodruff's analysis of Russia's economic evolution focuses on the demonetization issue, placing current developments in a comprehensive historical and political economic framework. He marks the key shifting point as October 1993 when electric power companies first stopped being able to collect debts in cash and then stopped paying their own fuel suppliers. Up until that point, they had mechanisms for extracting money from customers as long as those customers were legally holding money in some way (in banks, for example). In the fall of 1993, however, Russian industry basically ran out of money, and the electric power companies could no longer collect.[7]

Once this happened, a system of "surrogate money"—basically tradable debt—began to develop. When one firm could not pay another, it would instead issue a *veksel* or IOU. These had a nominal ruble value, the amount of the debt, and could be traded as a sort of money. Because they are in fact worth less than their nominal ruble value, they are, in accordance with Gresham's Law, preferable to the use of real cash money to settle debts.[8]

Vadim Radaev argues that restrictive monetary policy by the federal government is in part to blame for at least one aspect of demonetization: the various money substitutes that are issued by regional

---

[5]Breslauer et al., "Russia at the End of Yel'tsin's Presidency."

[6]Vladimir Popov, "Exchange Rate Policy After the Currency Crisis: Walking the Tightrope," PONARS, 2000.

[7]Woodruff, *Money Unmade: Barter and the Fate of Russian Capitalism.*

[8]Ibid.

governments, banks, and enterprises. In a 2000 paper, he wrote that more than half of transactions among business partners were carried out through barter and mutual offsetting. Moreover, he cited official data to note that only about one-half of nominal tax payments are collected at all, and only one-third is collected in monetary form.[9]

Clifford G. Gaddy and Barry Ickes describe Russia's current economic system as a "virtual economy," one in which value is destroyed rather than created. They trace the problem less to the legacy of the Soviet system and more to the effects of "incomplete" shock therapy (the notion that a quick, albeit painful transition to a market economy is the best mechanism for reform). The Soviet component, they argue, is the industrial sector that was inherited from the USSR. A large number of firms produce goods, but because the inputs into production are more valuable than the outputs, value is destroyed rather than created in production. To survive, the enterprise turns to strategies such as trading goods that cannot be sold on the market for other goods or services or for tax offsets. Barter and nonmonetary payment can also make the cost of the inputs lower. Of course, this creates disincentives for firms to restructure in more economically efficient ways, and the short-term effectiveness of these methods encourages others to imitate them. As barter becomes more common, even firms that can in principle afford to pay cash will, as Woodruff also notes, prefer to use the cheaper barter mechanism.[10]   Moreover, "relational capital"—the personal relationships that helped the Soviet economy function—support this system as well by smoothing the way for barter, other noncash payments, and arrears.[11]

Richard Ericson's analysis, introduced in the previous chapter, focuses on the links between these factors and economic regionalization (others note this aspect as well, but Ericson highlights it). He describes Russia's market structure as fragmented along the political and administrative boundaries that reflect Soviet patterns rather

---

[9]Vadim Radaev, "Consolidation of the Russian State and Economic Policy Scenarios Under Putin," PONARS, 2000.

[10]Gaddy and Ickes, *Stability and Disorder: An Evolutionary Analysis of Russia's Virtual Economy.*

[11]Ibid.

than actual opportunities. The social networks are further supported by the absence of legal protection, a weak banking system, and arbitrary taxation (among other factors).[12]

A Marxist take on Russian economic development is provided by Kotz, who argues that the Russian economy is not now, nor is it on the path to becoming, a capitalist system—one in which a capitalist mode of production is dominant. He argues that key aspects of capitalism are missing in Russia, including enterprises that produce commodities, subsistence wages paid to workers, and competition to sell commodities on the market. Although Russia has a market, it is a distorted/partial one characterized by barter and money surrogates, deliveries despite continued nonpayment, and workers paid in goods rather than wages. Rather than being paid subsistence wages, workers survive on production of food or products outside of the workplace (e.g., private garden plots). From their workplace they receive the benefits established during communist times: health and child care, education, etc. Production in the Russian economy is therefore not production for sale, but rather a mechanism to keep workers employed and traditional industrial relationships functioning.[13]

Moreover, Kotz argues, the new wealthy in Russia are not capitalists in that they are not growing wealthy off the surplus value of production by labor but rather through the export of oil and gas (which, in Marxist terms, is not fully capitalist because the infrastructure was preexisting and the assets are free or cheap, although oil and gas are sold at market rates), rent from ownership of land and buildings in urban areas, and loans of funds to the state itself, via the purchase of high-yield government bonds. Thus, a large portion of the new wealth comes from government budgets and the foreign aid that helps support them. Other sources of funds include merchant profits from trade; speculation in foreign currencies, precious metals, and securities; revenue skimmed from enterprises that are not making a profit; extortion; and theft of public funds, such as the disappeared $1 billion in aid money appropriated by the Duma for Chechnya re-

---

[12]Breslauer et al., "Russia at the End of Yel'tsin's Presidency."

[13]Kotz, "Is Russia Becoming Capitalist?"

construction after the 1994–1996 war and the diverted $30 million of a $90 million World Bank loan to Russia.[14]

Thus, Kotz argues, Russia's economic system is best characterized as not capitalist but "predatory/extractive," where income stems from raw materials, past labor in Soviet years (which created the infrastructure), and foreign wage labor. Moreover, the new wealthy do not reinvest their earnings in the Russian economy but rather send them abroad to banks or purchase luxury goods.[15] In doing so, as Brada suggests, they are largely responding to the incentives created by the Russian system, in which there are no real legal guarantees for property rights. A fear that one's firm and property may be renationalized should it seem expedient to the government in the future is entirely reasonable.[16]

Of course, the new wealthy are a very small segment of the population. The gap between rich and poor is widening. Twenty years ago in the Soviet Union, the wealthiest 10 percent of the population had slightly over three times the income of the poorest 10 percent. Today, the income of the wealthiest is almost 14 times that of the poorest, according to Russian government statistics. UN numbers are even higher: a factor of 23.[17] Many of Russia's poor are the elderly. Thirty percent of Russia's population was below the poverty line in 2000; the figure for 2001 was 27 percent and that for the first quarter of 2002 was 33 percent.[18] Another 50 percent or so, which includes most public sector doctors, teachers, etc., waver between poverty and the small middle-class stratum.[19] The situation is particularly dire outside the biggest cities, where many factories have ceased to function and months-long wage arrears are commonplace (the size of wage arrears varies by region, but the amount for the

---

[14]Ibid.

[15]Ibid.

[16]Breslauer et al., "Russia at the End of Yel'tsin's Presidency."

[17]Margaret Mary Henry, "A Modest Bourgeoisie Buds in Russia," *Christian Science Monitor*, February 4, 2002.

[18]"Russian Salaries Grow, Unemployment Falls—State Statistics Committee," *Johnson's Russia List* (Interfax), December 27, 2001; "33 Percent of Russians Live in Poverty," *Johnson's Russian List* (AP), June 1, 2002 (May 31, 2002).

[19]Henry, "A Modest Bourgeoisie Buds in Russia."

nation as a whole stood at $1.1 million in February 2002).[20] Survey data suggest that almost 50 percent of Russians perceive themselves and their families as struggling financially, and many take out loans for everyday expenses and view their savings as a mechanism for hedging against the possibility of job loss or wage arrears.[21]

While poverty among all age groups in Russia increased in the early to mid-1990s, the elderly were particularly hard-hit, with a tenfold increase in those living in poverty from 1993 to 1996 (as opposed to the fourfold increase for the rest of the population).[22] The average pension in Russia is below subsistence.[23] Youth are also disproportionately poor and disadvantaged. According to Russia's National Center for Preventative Medicine, Russia now has about one million seriously neglected children and 200,000 homeless children.[24]

Russian efforts at poverty alleviation have been limited by lack of funds and capacity. Lilia Ovtcharova provides an assessment of Russian social benefits to the poor. She writes that social benefits exist—indeed are widespread, with most Russians eligible for some form of assistance—but with a share of total population income of not more than 3 percent, they are not significant contributors. When social support to the poor is provided, it is rarely financial but more often consists of meals, packages, clothing, and housing. The costs for these supports are usually borne by the regions, which apply their own definition of poverty, usually at 50–70 percent of subsistence.[25]

---

[20]"Wage Arrears Grow," *RFE/RL Newsline*, Vol. 6, No. 32, Part I, February 19, 2002; "Russian Industrial Output Up in 2001," *Johnson's Russia List* (AP), January 19, 2002.

[21]Julie DaVanzo and Clifford Grammich, *Dire Demographics: Population Trends in the Russian Federation*, Santa Monica, California: RAND, 2001; Lilia Ovtcharova, "What Kind of Poverty Alleviation Policy Does Russia Need?" Russian-European Centre for Economic Policy, Moscow, 2001.

[22]DaVanzo and Grammich, *Dire Demographics*, p. 66.

[23]"Russian Salaries Grow, Unemployment Falls—State Statistics Committee."

[24]Jeremy Brantsen, "Russia: Poor Fitness of Conscripts Points to Public Health Crisis," *Johnson's Russia List*, January 17, 2002.

[25]Ovtcharova, "What Kind of Poverty Alleviation Policy Does Russia Need?"

CAPITAL FLIGHT

In this environment, it is not surprising that capital flight has been a consistent problem for Russia's troubled economy over the last decade. Flight takes the form both of purchases of foreign assets by Russian residents and of money siphoned off (showing up as errors and omissions in balance of payments accounts) and sent abroad.[26] As of April 2000, U.S. Treasury, International Monetary Fund (IMF), and other estimates suggested that over $100 billion in funds had left Russia over the past decade. After a drop in 1998 and 1999, preliminary figures for 2000 suggested that capital flight was approaching the 1996 high of $39 billion/year. By January 2002, illegal capital flight was estimated at $1 billion to $1.5 billion monthly.[27] On one hand, recent capital flight coincides with massive improvement in current account balances and helps keep inflation down—the Central Bank cannot effectively sterilize monetary inflow (this issue is discussed in more detail later); on the other hand, at a rate of over 10 percent of Russian gross domestic product (GDP), capital flight from the country is many times that elsewhere in the world (it is under 3 percent of GDP in both Mexico and South Korea).[28]

Capital flight in the long term translates into tax evasion, depriving the government of needed revenue with which to invest in the country or pay foreign debt, thus hurting the national credit. The low private and public investment it implies contributes to the deterioration of Russia's industrial base. And it provides numerous opportunities for organized criminal groups who coordinate the financial transfers involved.[29]

Early privatization mechanisms and pervasive corruption helped make it possible for much Russian wealth to escape the country. Manipulation of commodity export prices was one way in which

---

[26]Breslauer et al., "Russia at the End of Yel'tsin's Presidency."

[27]"Illegal Capital Flight Put at Up to $1.5 bln per Month," *Johnson's Russia List* (AP), January 23, 2002.

[28]Clifford G. Gaddy and Barry W. Ickes, "The Virtual Economy and Economic Recovery in Russia," *Transition Newsletter*, Vol. 12, No. 1, February–March 2001; Mark Kramer, "Capital Flight and Russian Economic Reform," PONARS, 2000.

[29]Kramer, "Capital Flight and Russian Economic Reform."

large amounts of unreported revenue could be accumulated. These funds were then transferred abroad.

Capital flight today tends to be through two approaches. One is to set artificially low prices when negotiating export contracts. The exporter declares a lower price for the goods exported than the buyer paid and keeps the difference (or splits it with the buyer). Because inspections are rare and there is no legal mechanism to force the inspection of most contracts, this sort of behavior can be difficult to interdict. The second approach is to use a "one-day" firm, set up to carry out a specific transaction or set of transactions and then dissolved. Because the firm no longer exists, it is impossible to investigate or to tax it. Some 16,000 export contracts reportedly passed through one-day firms in Moscow in 1999 alone.[30]

CRIME, CORRUPTION, AND THE SHADOW ECONOMY

In a recent report, the Russian newspaper *Trud* cited "expert" estimates of the gray (extralegal, such as legal enterprises hiding profits; or the one-third of respondents to a recent poll who admitted having an "informal" source of income[31]) economy at $50 billion for 2001. The report noted that the outright criminal economy comprised another $40–60 billion. The paper cited tax police chief Mikhail Fradkov as estimating the shadow economy (which combines the illegal and extralegal economies) at nearly 40 percent of Russia's economy as a whole, compared to 7–16 percent of the economies of European Union (EU) countries.[32] Ministry of Internal Affairs (MVD) statisticians also estimate that nearly half of Russia's GDP was produced illegally (although other government organizations estimate the shadow economy's share at only half that level). As already noted, not all, and most likely far from most, of this is illegal or criminal dealings per se; much is probably accounted for by nonpayment of taxes and barter relationships between firms (and the aforementioned one-day firms, which are an excellent mechanism

---

[30]Ibid.

[31]Henry, "A Modest Bourgeoisie Buds in Russia."

[32]Vitaly Golovachev, "Invisible Octopus," *Trud*, January 10, 2002.

for avoiding taxes[33]), but organized crime also plays a role. According to the MVD, half of Russia's banks and 80 percent of its joint ventures may be tied to criminal groups.[34] According to the Procurator General's office, up to 60 percent of Russian firms and organizations are controlled by organized crime groups.[35] One expert estimates the number of such groups operating on Russian Federation territory to be at least 3000.[36] A 1994 study estimated that 70–80 percent of private banks and businesses spend 10–20 percent of revenues on protection payments.[37]

Russian sources are consistent in reporting that bribery and corruption are commonplace throughout society, almost a norm of daily life. A study by Mehnaz S. Safavian, Douglas H. Graham, and Claudio Gonzalez-Vega notes that corruption functions regressively: large firms see it as a cost of gaining advantage, while for smaller firms, bribes are a tax that they pay more on than do larger firms. Moreover, for those smaller firms, bribery increases rather than decreases transaction costs, requiring more time to be spent with officials for very little gain.[38] In the *Trud* account, presidential economic advisor Andrei Illarionov is quoted as saying that corruption is becoming "institutionalized" in Russian society.[39] Indeed, some 6500 cases of bribe-taking were disclosed in 1999, and only 5–8 percent of those accused of taking bribes are convicted and imprisoned. Such figures have led many to call for increased penalties for bribe-taking and more forceful prosecution. However, as Vadim Radaev points out, a more successful approach might involve seeking to limit the incentives for officials to accept bribes, for instance by limiting the number of economic activities subject to government oversight

---

[33]Ibid.

[34]L. Kosals, "The shadow economy as an attribute of Russian capitalism" (in Russian), *Voprosy Ekonomiki*, No. 10, 1998, pp. 59–60; V. Medvedev, "Problems of Russia's Economic Security," *Russian Social Science Review*, Vol. 39, No. 6, November–December 1998, p. 18.

[35]Golovachev, "Invisible Octopus."

[36]Medvedev, "Problems of Russia's Economic Security."

[37]Kotz, "Is Russia Becoming Capitalist?"

[38]Mehnaz S. Safavian, Douglas H. Graham, and Claudio Gonzalez-Vega, "Corruption and Microenterprises in Russia," *World Development*, Vol. 29, No. 7, 2001.

[39]Golovachev, "Invisible Octopus."

or restrictions (which provide opportunity and incentive for corruption), centralizing the surveillance functions that do exist, and improving the legal framework that governs official interaction with economic entities.[40]

Radaev provides a nuanced assessment of organized crime in Russia in an October 1998 paper in the Russian journal *Voprosy Ekonomiki*. He reports that a survey of businesses throughout Russia suggests that the scope of criminal involvement in the day-to-day Russian economy, though high, is in fact often overstated. The perceptions of the prevalence of crime far outweigh actual reports of dealings with criminals.[41]

Even the lower number remains worrisome, however. In the survey, 42 percent of business managers reported some personal experience with the use of force in their professional life. Radaev estimates that the actual scope of criminal involvement in business is on the order of 15 percent (presumably of transactions), but he argues that this figure suggests that the phenomenon is sufficiently widespread that force has become "routinized" in Russian economic life—a part of day-to-day experience.[42] Such routinization may help explain why people's perceptions of criminal involvement may be higher than its actuality.

Radaev's data also suggest that even the possibility of seeking assistance from police or other law enforcement carries an element of force or criminal activity. By and large, only those who have personal ties to police or government officials receive much in the way of support from them. In the absence of such ties, criminal protection may seem an attractive alternative option.[43]

In fact, some argue that Russian security organizations have simply taken over from organized criminal groups to become another form of organized crime that promises protection to businessmen. There

---

[40]Radaev, "Consolidation of the Russian State and Economic Policy Scenarios Under Putin."

[41]V. Radaev, "On the role of force in Russian business relationships," *Voprosy Ekonomiki*, No. 10, October 1998.

[42]Ibid.

[43]Ibid.

are reportedly links between security forces (including the Federal Security Service [FSB], and GUBOP—the MVD's organized crime unit) and various criminal groups, in some cases involving protection for the criminal group against threats posed by other security forces.[44] Noted analyst Anders Åslund is quoted in a recent *Christian Science Monitor* article on the growth of the middle class in Russia as saying, "The security police, the tax police and other law enforcement agents are the organized crime in Russia today, so you have to get the state-sponsored organized crime under control."[45]

TURNAROUND?

Since the 1998 crisis, and especially over the last two years, Russia has appeared to experience an economic resurgence. Popov notes drops in nonmonetary payments and money substitutes since 1998 as well as a drop in industrial arrears from over 64 percent in August 1998 to under 30 percent in the middle of 2000. The proportion of transactions based on barter has halved to 26 percent.[46]

Production of goods and services in the core sectors of the Russian economy, an indicator of economic growth as a whole, was 10.2 percent in 2000.[47] The average monthly salary in Russia grew by 46.2 percent in 2001 (though it then dropped slightly in the first month of 2002[48]). Factoring in inflation, according to the State Statistics Committee, this translates into real growth of 12 percent. Pensions have increased, although they remain below subsistence. As of December 1, 2001, arrears had decreased to 34.8 billion rubles, a 3.1 billion ruble drop since the start of the year.[49]

---

[44]See Roustam Kaliyev, "Russia's Organized Crime: A Typology," *Johnson's Russia List* (Eurasia.net), February 5, 2002.

[45]Henry, "A Modest Bourgeoisie Buds in Russia."

[46]Popov, "Exchange Rate Policy After the Currency Crisis: Walking the Tightrope."

[47]"Russian Economy Grows 5.7 Percent in 2001," *Johnson's Russia List* (Interfax), January 23, 2002.

[48]"Russia Publishes Population Figures," *Johnson's Russia List* (ITAR-TASS), February 23, 2002.

[49]"Russian Salaries Grow, Unemployment Falls—State Statistics Committee."

The number of unemployed in Russia dropped as well, from 7.1 million in January 2001 to 6.3 million in December of that year.[50] The economy continued to grow in 2001. While the 9 percent growth rate of 2000 in industrial production was not sustained, 4.9 percent growth was achieved.[51] Growth in core sector production dropped to 5.7 percent.[52] A total of 961.3 billion rubles was collected in taxes in 2001, 8.1 percent more than the budget target of the previous year.[53]

Another improvement indicator is the existence of a small but growing middle class in Russia, estimated by one research agency at 7 percent of the overall population and 20 percent of the Moscow population. It is composed of educated homeowners with incomes of $150–$2000 a month, probably underreported because of the tendency to hide earnings and significant consumer spending.[54]

Self-employment has also grown, mostly in the form of trade, sales, street vending, taxi and truck driving, construction, and various services, such as medical, accounting, security, cleaning, sewing, astrology, and the like. The self-employed are disproportionately young, male, and well-educated.[55]

However, there are those who believe that these improvements are not sustainable. Gaddy and Ickes argue that the current recovery is a result of external factors, particularly high oil prices, rather than the institutional change that would make lasting change possible. Moreover, the virtual economy described above remains in place and continues to create disincentives to real reform. They argue that while ruble depreciation has made Russian goods more competitive, the drop in household income and consumption (compared to 1997–1998, it is up slightly from 2000–2001) suggests a negative undercurrent to these positive figures. Gaddy and Ickes go on to say that

---

[50]Ibid.

[51]"Russian Industrial Output Up in 2001."

[52]"Russian Economy Grows 5.7 percent in 2001."

[53]"Russian Industrial Output Up in 2001."

[54]Henry, "A Modest Bourgeoisie Buds in Russia."

[55]Theodore Gerber, "The Development of Self-Employment in Russia," PONARS, 2001.

barter has decreased only because cash has become cheaper, and, if anything, economic growth is being used as an excuse not to carry out reforms. [56]

While Gaddy and Ickes may tend to understate the real positive changes that are visible in the Russian economy, they are right to question their sustainability and the need for more fundamental reforms. Economic growth based fundamentally on the high price of oil cannot be a recipe for long-term success, particularly when oil production and investment in Russian oil industry infrastructure continue to lag.[57] Data presented by Vladimir Popov bear this out. He notes that Russian investment remains low and agricultural and housing subsidies high. Changes in these areas would be difficult and unpopular, but they are necessary for sustainable success. Russia also needs to fundamentally improve its legal and tax framework to attract foreign direct investment, levels of which remain very low in Russia, especially when compared on a per capita level with states such as Hungary or Azerbaijan (although it should be noted that the Azerbaijani oil sector accounts for a good deal of the investment).[58] As Mark Kramer points out, the current system, with its lack of protection for private property or contract enforcement, regulated securities markets, mechanisms to protect shareholder rights, or effective banks, is unlikely to attract foreign or domestic investors.[59]

Certainly the need for tax reform is clear from both the foreign and the domestic perspective. In January 2002, the Moscow office chief of the federal tax police service reported that 60 percent of Russian firms and institutions do not pay taxes or other duties. These firms are predominately in the energy, credit and financial, real estate, consumer trade, and export-import sectors.[60]

The unsustainability of Russia's current situation is particularly disturbing given the analysis in David Woodruff's examination of how

---

[56]Gaddy and Ickes, "The Virtual Economy and Economic Recovery in Russia."

[57]"Russian Industrial Output Up in 2001."

[58]Vladimir Popov, "Why the Russian Economy Is Unlikely to Become a New 'Asian Tiger,'" PONARS, 2000.

[59]Kramer, "Capital Flight and Russian Economic Reform."

[60]"Tax Police: 60 Percent of Russian Business Entities Fail to Pay Taxes," *RFE/RL Newsline*, Vol. 6, No. 5, Part I, January 9, 2002.

Russia is able to maintain a weak ruble when oil prices are high—the key to its recent success. He argues that the Russian Central Bank has been artificially keeping the ruble weak by buying up the dollars that appear in the economy from oil sales. As a result, far more rubles are released into the economy, which then need to be sterilized to prevent ruble appreciation. To date, the Finance Ministry has been doing this by holding on to large deposits instead of spending to pay off debts on older, defunct government bonds or by buying dollars from the Central Bank to pay off foreign debt. Woodruff argues that Russia is avoiding paying off debts because it fears that to do so would damage its negotiating position on debt rescheduling.[61]

The recent reversals in Russia's phenomenal 2000–2001 growth provide evidence of this less rosy picture. If the average Russian income, adjusted for inflation, grew by 8.5 percent between January 2001 and January 2002, it also dropped by 36.2 percent between December 2001 and January 2002.[62] How the rest of 2002 goes will provide key evidence of whether Russia's economy is on its way up or its way down. However, there is clearly considerable cause for pessimism.

Thus, whether or not one accepts Gaddy and Ickes' formulation of the "virtual economy," they are right to argue that Russia's economy today, the starting point for current reforms, is a long way from the 1991–1992 economy, and has its own pathologies, challenges, and problems. They are also correct in identifying an important roadblock to reform—that many more individuals, groups, and firms stand to gain from preserving the status quo than was true ten years ago.[63]

Under the best of circumstances, such a situation would make economic reform a tremendous political challenge. In Russia, where economics and politics have become fundamentally intertwined, with economic and political interests consistently engaged in inefficient but mutually profitable side deals and agreements, the knots may take years to unravel, if they can be unraveled at all. There

---

[61]David Woodruff, "Too Much of a Good Thing? High Oil Prices and Russian Monetary Policy," PONARS, 2000.

[62]"Russia Publishes Population Figures."

[63]Gaddy and Ickes, *Stability and Disorder: An Evolutionary Analysis of Russia's Virtual Economy.*

is a temptation to seek to solve these problems with the same sort of centralized, regulatory, top-down approach that the Putin administration has taken to the threat of political regionalization.[64] If Russia's goal is a market system, this could be very dangerous. The key is to establish structures that favor investment and market relations, and to shift the incentives away from extralegal and short-term activities. Legal and tax reform are the first steps, but the real challenge will be finding a way to reverse the processes that have begun to institutionalize illegality and force in the Russian economic system. In the meantime, the disparate levels of economic reform in various regions and the varying economic indicators among them create the potential for economic grievances on the part of poorer regions. As already noted, this can feed into interregional, and, insofar as the regions are divided along ethnic lines, interethnic discord, as well as create further tension between the regions and the center.

---

[64]Kramer notes proposals by Federal Currency Export Control Service Chief Aleksandr Gromov to implement intrusive restrictions as well as proposed laws on capital flight that would similarly rely on regulation rather than market forces. Kramer, "Capital Flight and Russian Economic Reform."

Chapter Four

RUSSIA'S POLITICAL FUTURE: WHITHER DEMOCRACY AND FREEDOM?

In one sense, Russia is fundamentally and unquestionably a democracy. Free elections are held, including the presidential election that cemented Vladimir Putin in power in 2000. Politicians are concerned about their prospects for reelection and behave accordingly. Federal law requires that elections be contested; candidates cannot legally run unopposed. If the people of Russia can be accused of voting on personalities rather than issues, and, indeed, of being insufficiently well-informed when they cast their ballots, they are no different in this from the citizens of most other countries, including the United States. If business interests can be thought to sometimes hold a bit too much sway over political figures, once again, Russia cannot be said to be alone in such a pathology.

Of course, as with everything in Russia, the situation varies from region to region. Elections in Nizhny Novgorod and Novosibirsk suggest competitive democracy, while Bashkortostan, Primorsky Krai, Tatarstan, and Kalmykia seem far less pluralistic. Despite federal law, the leaders of Tatarstan and Kalmykia ran unopposed in recent elections. Moreover, according to Henry Hale, incumbents are winning more and more elections throughout Russia, with increasing shares of the popular vote—an ominous phenomenon in a country where such statistics are reminiscent of the days of Soviet rule.[1]

---

[1] Henry Hale, "The State of Democratization in Russia in Light of the Elections," PONARS, 2000.

Another indicator of democratization is the presence and role of political parties. Kathryn Stoner-Weiss finds parties in Russia to be fairly well-ingrained on the national level, with solid electoral blocks behind the Communists, Yabloko, Union of Right Wing Forces, and the Liberal Democratic Party of Russia (LDPR) (there is also usually a party that represents the interests of the president, which generally enjoys significant representation in the Duma). Although other parties are small and fleeting, those noted here have survived for sufficiently long and with sufficient success to suggest that parties can be viable in Russian politics. Whatever one may think of these groups' platforms, and the LDPR is particularly unsavory, they consistently command a reputable share of the vote in national elections.[2]

At the local level, however, Stoner-Weiss finds that the parties are weak. While the Communists, LDPR, and Yabloko are represented in some regional legislatures, most power is concentrated in local political machines. Regional elites frequently change party affiliation and election rules, which are controlled by the local leadership, and tend to favor single-mandate rather than mixed or proportional representation systems. Registration rules have been jiggered to prevent specific individuals from running, and local elites' control of media can play an important role in election campaigns. Rent-seeking behavior is also common in relations between local officials and business interests, in which each seeks a variety of gains through ties with the other. Stoner-Weiss argues that the reality of political parties at the national level combined with their weakness at the local level indicates that party penetration in the regions is being actively and purposefully prevented.[3]

Democracy itself aside, there is growing concern that Vladimir Putin's Russia is increasingly unfree. Print and electronic media throughout Russia have long been controlled either by the state/region or by business interests, which provided alternative (if still biased) perspectives. Whether the replacement of the management (and effectively, the journalistic staff) of the independent NTV television station was motivated by a "personal vendetta" on the part

---

[2]Ibid.

[3]Kathryn Stoner-Weiss, "The Limited Reach of Russia's Party System: Under-Institutionalization in the Provinces," PONARS, 2000.

of President Putin against media baron Vladimir Gusinsky, a desire to silence an opposing voice, or legal/financial reasons, the result has been an increased perception among the press that free speech does not fully exist in Russia, and that police and government organs may be used to silence critical or independent media.[4] The more recent closing of TV-6, to which many of the NTV journalists had fled, corroborates these fears throughout Russia's media and scholarly society. Indeed, TV-6, closed down in early 2002 in accordance with a law that was rarely enforced and recently repealed (although still in effect long enough to close the television station), was a particularly egregious and difficult-to-defend situation.[5] Moreover, a smoking gun can perhaps be seen in the comments of Mikhail Lesin, the Kremlin's point man on the press and the media, who has said publicly that he feels that the media is more dangerous to the state than vice versa. Although Lesin was not directly involved in the closing of TV-6, he was connected to the NTV shutdown.[6]

Interestingly, after TV-6 was shut down Lesin discussed the dangerous implications of regional political and business control of the media, which he argued should not be used to reflect local political and business interests. In the same speech, he stated that business control over the national media had declined. This provides some interesting insight into Lesin's view of what is indeed dangerous and suggests that he saw, or would like to portray, NTV and TV-6 as the mouthpieces of hostile business interests rather than as examples of free press.[7]

Lesin's view is shared by at least some lawmakers. Late in 2001, the Duma approved draft amendments that, if signed into law, would ban the use of media and computer information networks in the service of "propaganda," "terrorism," or "extremism." Moreover, the media would be prohibited from publishing or broadcasting any statements by the undefined terrorists or extremists or, indeed, by

---

[4]Hale, "The State of Democratization in Russia in Light of the Elections"; Nicholson, "Putin's Russia: Slowing the Pendulum Without Stopping the Clock."

[5]"Lesin's Laser," *Wall Street Journal Europe*, December 6, 2001.

[6]Ibid.

[7]Clara Ferreira-Marques, "Russian Media Freedoms Still Uncertain—Minister," *Johnson's Russia List* (Reuters), February 6, 2002.

anyone who might be seeking to support them or to prevent or limit counterterrorist efforts. As Lisa Vronskaya notes, this vague language, if passed into law, would have tremendous implications for freedom of the press and free speech.[8]

Concerns were raised again by February 2002 reports of draft proposals from the MVD to restrict internet access. These reports were denied by the ministry, although the reporter who initially broadcast the story on radio station Ekho Moskvy continued to insist that it was confirmed by sources within the MVD.[9] Such an effort would be in keeping with previous Russian government actions, such as the SORM (System of Operative and Investigative Procedures) regulations issued in the 1990s to give the FSB access to telephone, cellular, and internet communication throughout Russia. The mechanics and effectiveness of activities pursued in accordance with SORM are unclear, as is the status of the regulations themselves (they have been challenged in court).[10]

That the press has been effectively muzzled in at least some cases is supported largely by anecdotal evidence, as the timescale is too short for anything more definitive. One example is the December 19, 2001, press conference by Tatyana Kasatkina and Oleg Orlov, leaders of the human rights group Memorial. At the press conference, Kasatkina and Orlov accused Russian army and special services of creating death squads in Chechnya and torturing to death Chechen prisoners. According to Vronskaya, not a single Russian press organization picked up the story until after it was published, on December 20, in a Spanish newspaper. At that point, Russian press reports appeared, citing the Spanish paper.[11]

---

[8]Lisa Vronskaya, "Duma Approves Amendments Curtailing Press Freedoms," *Johnson's Russia List* (Gazeta.ru), December 20, 2001.

[9]"Author of Internet Censorship in Russia Article Comments on His Sources," *Johnson's Russia List* (BBC Monitoring, Ekho Moskvy), 10:26 am, February 2, 2002; "Interior Ministry Denies Reports of Plans to Restrict Access to Internet," *Johnson's Russia List* (Interfax), 10:26 am, February 2, 2002.

[10]Information on SORM, including text of the regulations issued, is posted by *Institute of Freedom: Moscow Libertarium* (cited February 22, 2002); available from www.libertarium.ru.

[11]Vronskaya, "Duma Approves Amendments Curtailing Press Freedoms."

The Russian public, somewhat disturbingly, appears largely uncon-
cerned by these developments and has failed to protest against the
government regarding the closure of these television stations and
other media organs.[12]

President Putin's background in the KGB and his reliance on advisors
and aides with a similar background creates additional concern on
the part of many Russians and Russia-watchers about the implications for freedom and democracy. Indeed, Putin has placed a number of high-ranked intelligence officers in various jobs, including the
Ministry of Defense (MoD) and the MVD. In July 2001, he put an FSB
general in charge of a newly created directorate for electronic intelligence collection and the fight against high-technology crime.[13]

Additional concerns are raised by the judicial pursuit in the past two
years of analysts, journalists, and whistle-blowers who are tried on
charges of espionage and treason. Military journalist Grigory Pasko,
who was looking into nuclear-waste handling by the Pacific Fleet,
was accused of spying for Japan. A similar case involved naval officer
Aleksandr Nikitin, who publicly revealed unsafe navy practices in regard to nuclear materials. Analyst Igor Sutyagin, of the Institute for
USA and Canada Research, remains in prison on remand, charged
with passing classified nuclear data to the United States and Great
Britain. Sutyagin's attorneys argue that he has never had access to
classified information. These and similar trials (of, for example,
American Edmond Pope, Russian scientist Valentin Danilov, Russian
diplomat Valentin Moiseev[14]) are carried out at least partially in secret, with defense lawyers often not given access to some of the evidence against their clients. Together with the harassment that re-
searchers in the defense and/or nuclear fields have increasingly
faced from the police and FSB, such trials can be seen as a concerted

---

[12]Petrov, "Policization Versus Democratization."

[13]"Putin Installs Intelligence Officers in Interior Ministry," *RFE/RL Newsline*, Vol. 5,
No. 129, Part I, July 11, 2001.

[14]A list of cases, with information about each, is provided by Digital Freedom Network
at *Similar Cases* [Internet edition] (cited February 22, 2002), http://www.
prava.org/similar/index.htm#similar.

campaign to pressure those who would research and report on sensitive topics to cease their efforts.[15]

The co-optation of the judicial branch, as well as law enforcement, is a disturbing trend. Nikolai Petrov, in fact, argues that "Putin's reform is directed primarily at strengthening control by the police over the society," which he terms "policization." He presents little in the way of evidence to support his argument that the police and secret police have increasing control over all aspects of society, including the military and elites, but his argument represents a view shared by many Russians.[16]

Certainly the trends in the media, in the courts, and in efforts to control the internet are disturbing. As the discussion of political parties and elections demonstrates, democracy in Russia is far from entrenched, and freedom seems even less so. Moreover, all of these aspects vary to some extent by region. The lack of public outcry at newly imposed restrictions and limits on free speech and the press suggests that, up to a certain point, the majority of the Russian people may be willing to trade freedom for the stability that they hope President Putin will bring. And, indeed, autocratic states can be stable, as witness the Soviet Union. But constraints on personal freedoms will be, even as they are already, reflected in constraints on economic freedom and very likely in Russia's capacity for economic growth (although, of course, there are models for economic growth under autocratic systems). Perhaps most important, because so many of Putin's efforts and reforms are tied up with him, personally, as leader, whether their direction is autocratic or democratic, it is difficult to judge whether his successor will follow the same path. If

---

[15]David Hoffman, "Russia Places Scholar on Trial for Espionage," *Washington Post,* December 27, 2000; "No End to Spy Mania in Russia," *Jamestown Foundation Monitor,* Vol. 7, Issue 2, January 3, 2001; "Researcher's Espionage Trial Postponed," *RFE/RL Newsline,* Vol. 4, No. 248, Part I, December 27, 2000; "Rights Seemingly Under Assault in Spy Trials," *Jamestown Foundation Monitor,* Vol. 6, Issue 221, November 28, 2000; "Russian Arms Researcher Called Spy," *Johnson's Russia List* (Associated Press), December 27, 2001; "Treason Trial of Russian Defense Analyst Set to Resume," *Jamestown Foundation Monitor,* Vol. 7, Issue 27, February 8, 2001; author discussions and interviews.

[16]Petrov, "Policization Versus Democratization."

Russia does move in the direction of personalized autocracy, it runs the risk that is faced by all personal autocracies—tremendous instability and danger when a succession takes place.

Chapter Five

THE PEOPLE OF RUSSIA: ASSET OR LIABILITY?

DEMOGRAPHICS[1]

There can be no doubt that the oppressiveness of the Soviet system created tremendous misery among the Russian people, the effects of which remain today. That said, the Communists should be given credit for imposing a far-ranging and efficient education system that quickly brought almost universal literacy to a nation that had had very limited access to education under previous regimes. Similarly, the Soviet socialized medical system, despite its drawbacks, provided medical care to many who might have lived shorter and even less pleasant lives without it. Unfortunately, the experience of the last ten years suggests that many of these gains, particularly in the health-care arena, are far from irreversible; Russia is facing a growing public health crisis and a series of critical demographic challenges.

The first of these challenges is population decline. Although the population had been urbanizing and its rates of growth shrinking consistently in parallel with the rest of the industrialized world before 1992, the patterns of today's decreasing birth rates and rising death rates suggest something outside the norm. Despite the significant influx of ethnic Russians from neighboring republics during the early to mid-1990s, over the past nine years Russia's population has

---

[1]This section draws heavily on the excellent report on Russian demographics by Julie DaVanzo and Clifford Grammich: *Dire Demographics: Population Trends in the Russian Federation.* The authors provide a wealth of information and readers are advised to consult their report.

shrunk by over 3 million people (458,400 during the first six months of 2001[2]).[3] Population forecasts are even grimmer. Russia's population today can be estimated at about 144 million.[4] Population projections for the Russian Federation in 2015 range from an optimistic assessment of 147.2 million to around 130 million.[5] By 2050, argues Murray Feshbach, a leading Western analyst of Russian society and environment, the Russian Federation could have a population as low as 80 million. For comparison purposes, it is projected that by 2050 the population of the United States will have *increased* by nearly 45 percent over current numbers. For Russia, the expectation (based on the low-end Feshbach estimate) over the same time period would be a *decline* of 45 percent.[6]

Migration rates are a factor in this decline. Immigration from other post-Soviet states helped moderate the decline caused by dropping birth and increasing death rates in the early 1990s. The rates of immigrants arriving from neighboring states rose steadily until 1994, and then remained at a lower but steady and positive rate until recently.[7] In the last year or two, however, immigration into Russia has dropped off.[8] These immigrants to Russia receive some assistance from the federal government, but services vary significantly by region. Moreover, immigrants tend to have difficulty finding employment and housing in Russia's strained economy, and the areas in which they cluster, many near the borders of Central Asian

---

[2]"Russian Population Continues to Decline," *RFE/RL Newsline*, Vol. 5, No. 158, Part I, August 21, 2001.

[3]Nail' Gaftulin, "Yet another crisis—a demographic one" (in Russian), *Krasnaya Zvezda*, June 5, 2000, Internet edition, www.redstar.ru; Alla Astakhova, "Scenarios of extinction" (in Russian), *Segodnya*, September 12, 2000, Internet edition, www.segodnya.ru/w3s.nsf/Contents/2000_203_news_text_astahoval.html.

[4]"Russia Publishes Population Figures."

[5]Astakhova.

[6]Murray Feshbach, "A Sick and Shrinking Nation," *Washington Post*, October 24, 1999, p. A23.

[7]Theodore Gerber, "Russia's Population Crisis: The Migration Dimension," PONARS, 2000.

[8]DaVanzo and Grammich, *Dire Demographics*; Paul Goble, "Russian Presence in Former Republics Declines," *RFE/RL Newsline Endnote*, Vol. 5, No. 149, Part I, August 8, 2001; Mikhail Tul'skiy, "The true face of the demographic catastrophe," *Nezavisimaya Gazeta*, July 19, 2001.

or Transcaucasus states, have higher than average rates of crime, unemployment, and illness.[9]   Thus, Russia cannot count on immigration to provide a continued alleviation of the overall drop in population.

The fact of population decline is not nearly as disturbing as its components. Russia's fertility rates (on average, 1.2 children born per woman per lifetime), while among the lowest in the world, are not dissimilar from fertility rates in Spain or Italy. Moreover, Russia's staggering abortion rate—at 70 percent of pregnancies one of the highest in the world—has been declining recently because of the greater availability of birth control. Although abortion was legal in the Soviet Union and remains legal in Russia, the stigma (medical records were public knowledge) led many women to seek illegal abortions, which often led to health problems or even death.[10]

The declining birth rate must be considered in conjunction with an increasing death rate, and, moreover, with the fact that the death rate has climbed disproportionately for one segment of the population—working-age men. If in the 1960s Soviet medicine helped attain life expectancies comparable to Western levels, the situation today suggests a frightening reversal of progress.[11] From a statistical perspective, Russian men born in 2000 can expect to live to be 58.9 years old. Women born that same year can expect to live to be 72. This is particularly significant in light of the fact that Russia is one of only eight countries (seven of them post-Soviet) with differences in life expectancy between women and men of over ten years.[12] Alcoholism, violence, and infectious and noninfectious diseases contributed to an estimated 2.8 million premature deaths in Russia between 1991 and 1998.[13] The link between the deaths of men and alcohol abuse is difficult to refute. Leading causes of male deaths—circulatory diseases, accidents, poisoning, and violence—are all correlated with high alcohol consumption. Moreover, DaVanzo and Grammich note that per capita alcohol consumption rates in Russia

---

[9]Gerber, "Russia's Population Crisis: The Migration Dimension."

[10]DaVanzo and Grammich, *Dire Demographics*, p. 25.

[11]DaVanzo and Grammich, *Dire Demographics*, pp. 50–51.

[12]DaVanzo and Grammich, *Dire Demographics*, pp. 37–48.

[13]Kotz, "Is Russia Becoming Capitalist?"

are above levels that the World Health Organization deems danger-ous. Traditional Russian drinking habits, which often involve ingest-ing large quantities of hard alcohol in a single sitting, are probably also a factor.[14] Further evidence lies in the far lower rates of alcohol-related death in Islamic parts of Russia, which also tend to have higher fertility rates.[15]

One aspect of these demographic trends is that Russia will see an in-creasing "graying" of its population in coming years, with steadily declining numbers of young people of working age generally and of men of military age in particular.[16] The Russian Federation's Security Council projects that by 2015 the number of people eligible for each year's military service call-up will nearly halve from 2000's 850,000 to 450,000.[17] Rather, more and more of the population will be made up of the elderly, and, if trends continue, predominantly the female elderly.[18] The Russian pension structure and medical-care system were not developed for such a contingency, and their deterio-ration over the past ten years makes them even less capable of re-sponding. As noted above, retirees are already an increasing propor-tion of Russia's poor.

Disease and illness are two more key components of what has been referred to as Russia's demographic crisis. The legacy of centralized health planning is a contributing factor in that it resulted in ineffi-cient investments in medical infrastructure and education. There are too many physicians in narrow specialties and not enough in general practice.[19] Increasing poverty is also a contributing factor. Many people cannot afford medical care, which was available at little or no cost throughout Soviet times.[20] It is telling that 40 percent of young men reporting for conscription were rejected last year because of poor physical or mental health. The more privileged in society can

---

[14]DaVanzo and Grammich, *Dire Demographics*, pp. 58–61.

[15]DaVanzo and Grammich, *Dire Demographics*, pp. 24, 37–48.

[16]DaVanzo and Grammich, *Dire Demographics*, pp. 71–74.

[17]"Russia's Dwindling Population Ensures Rigid Foreign Policy," April 13, 2000, Stratfor.com email publication.

[18]DaVanzo and Grammich, *Dire Demographics*, pp. 71–74.

[19]DaVanzo and Grammich, *Dire Demographics*, pp. 29–30.

[20]DaVanzo and Grammich, *Dire Demographics*, p. 62.

often find ways to avoid the draft, so that conscripts tend to reflect the poorest and least privileged segments of the population. Indeed, many young men receive the first physical examination of their lives when they report for service.[21]

Russia's medical system is not capable of handling high rates of disease effectively, yet it is repeatedly faced with the threat of an epidemic. For instance, in October 2001, First Deputy Health Minister Genadii Onishchenko reported that Russia had serious outbreaks of viral hepatitis.[22] Rising rates of tuberculosis are another indicator of the decline of Russia's health-care capacity. Tuberculosis in Russia kills more people today than any other infectious disease. The Red Cross estimates that 130,000 new cases of tuberculosis develop each year in Russia and 30,000 people annually die from the disease in that country.[23] This is a rate higher than that in China, Brazil, or Mexico and is three times the level of tuberculosis in Europe (and ten times the level in the United States or Canada).[24]

The high rates of tuberculosis reflect an increase in drug-resistant strains, arising in part from incomplete and inconsistent use of medication and treatment, the cost of treatment, and the unavailability of the individualized treatments used by Western doctors. According to a recent World Health Organization study, all those who had been treated for tuberculosis in their sample had developed multidrug-resistant forms of the disease resulting from poor treatment practices.[25] Rates this high have not been seen in Russia since the early 1970s. Tuberculosis is of particular concern in Russia's

---

[21]Brantsen, "Russia: Poor Fitness of Conscripts Points to Public Health Crisis."

[22]"Mortality Rates for Working-Age Males 'Weak Link' in Russia's Demographic Picture," *RFE/RL Newsline*, Vol. 5, No. 207, Part I, October 31, 2001.

[23]"...As Tuberculosis Remains a Major Health Concern," *RFE/RL Newsline*, Vol. 5, No. 223, Part I, November 27, 2001.

[24]DaVanzo and Grammich, *Dire Demographics*, pp. 51–55. It should be noted that Health Minister Yurii Shevchenko said in July 2001 that the numbers of tuberculosis cases had been inflated in an effort to increase foreign assistance, and the true numbers of Russian sufferers of the disease was not the 5 million commonly cited but only 200,000 ("Tuberculosis Figures Said Not as Bad as Reported," *RFE/RL Newsline*, Vol. 5, No. 130, Part I, July 12, 2001). While it is possible that the high-end numbers were, indeed, somewhat exaggerated, Shevchenko's estimate seems incredibly low.

[25]Nicholaas Eberstadt, "Russia: Too Sick to Matter?" *Policy Review*, June/July 1999, No. 95, pp. 3–22.

prison system. One million of Russia's 145 million population is in-carcerated. Nearly one in ten prisoners is infected with tuberculosis, 20 percent of them suffering from a multidrug-resistant strain.[26]

Also of concern is the rising rate of HIV infection, particularly be-cause Russian hospitals tend to lack modern AIDS drugs and equip-ment for treating AIDS patients. Although Russia reported fewer than 1000 AIDS deaths in 1999, a high underreporting rate can be as-sumed. DaVanzo and Grammich cite estimates of Russians living with HIV/AIDS that start at 130,000 and go up to 500,000, one mil-lion, or even higher.[27] The number of HIV cases reported in the first ten months of 2001—70,000—was 1.6 times the number reported in the first ten months of 2000, according to the Russian Federal Center for Prevention and Combating AIDS, which estimated the total for 2001 as potentially as high as 100,000.[28] In 2000, the number of people living with HIV/AIDS in the United States was 850,000,[29] but the estimates for Russia must be seen in light of what is probably significant underreporting and underdiagnosis of the disease.

HIV infection patterns in Russia reflect a somewhat different mode of infection from those in the United States or Europe. DaVanzo and Grammich note that most of Russia's reported HIV-positive popula-tion can be found in and around Moscow, St. Petersburg, and Irkutsk. It is disproportionately male and between the ages of 20 and 30. Intravenous drug use is believed to be a decisive factor in the spread of HIV in Russia. [30]

Indeed, drug abuse and addiction are yet another growing health challenge for Russia. In September 2001, President Putin described Russia's drug problem as sufficiently serious to threaten the coun-try's national security. Some 20 percent of Russian conscripts admit to having used drugs, while government estimates suggest that some

---

[26]DaVanzo and Grammich, *Dire Demographics*, pp. 51–55.

[27]DaVanzo and Grammich, *Dire Demographics*, p. 55.

[28]"Over 70,000 New HIV Cases Registered in Russia in 2001..." *RFE/RL Newsline*, Vol. 5, No. 223, Part I, November 27, 2001.

[29]DaVanzo and Grammich, *Dire Demographics*, p. 55.

[30]DaVanzo and Grammich, *Dire Demographics*, pp. 55–56.

80 percent of teenagers have experimented with illegal substances.[31] Moreover, the number of drug users registered in urban clinics increased by 600 percent between 1996 and 2001.[32] In 2000, government estimates of those registered between the ages of 13 and 25 alone topped 3 million.[33] Narcotics are an important component of Russia's illegal economy, at a rate of $1 billion/year. Russia is on the path of five major international drug trade channels: through the Baltic states, Europe, the Caucasus, Central Asia, and the Russian Far East.[34]

Like all else in Russia, the effects of the demographic and health-care crisis vary by region. To some extent, it is ethnically based: ethnic Russians are disproportionately affected by most of Russia's demographic problems. Only groups with high rates of emigration from Russia—Germans, Jews, and Ukrainians—show similar rates of population decline. DaVanzo and Grammich report that Russia's east and south (Siberia and the north Caucasus) have higher fertility rates than other parts of Russia. As noted above, Muslim regions tend to have higher fertility rates as well. Rural women continue to have slightly more children per capita than do urban women, although they, too, are reproducing below replacement level. [35]

ETHNICITY AND RACISM

Nationalism in Russia remains a sketchy issue. A definition of "Russian" that is not ethnically or imperially based may be a goal of many Russians, but ethnic allegiances remain strong and an effective mechanism to mobilize people in Russia. Moreover, the scapegoating of minority groups that often accompanies economic and political turmoil has been a consistent, if difficult to measure, aspect of life in Russia since independence. The extent to which scapegoating can

---

[31]Paul Goble, "Three Million Young Russians Addicted to Drugs," *RFE/RL Newsline*, Vol. 4, No. 146, Part I, August 1, 2000; "Putin Says Drug Problem Threatens Russian National Security," *RFE/RL Newsline*, Vol. 5, No. 185, Part I, October 1, 2001.

[32]"Registered Drug Users Increase Six Times Over Last Five Years," *RFE/RL Newsline*, Vol. 5, No. 135, Part I, July 19, 2001.

[33]Paul Goble, "Three Million Young Russians Addicted to Drugs."

[34]"Putin Says Drug Problem Threatens Russian National Security."

[35]DaVanzo and Grammich, *Dire Demographics*, pp. 2–9, 24–28.

translate into serious ethnic and/or regional conflict is uncertain, but the existence of ethnic tension suggests that the possibility is there.

Although President Putin appears to profess what Astrid Tuminez terms a "moderate statism" that defines as Russian all citizens of the Federation, some of his statements about Chechnya (to say nothing of his administration's actions in carrying out war there) suggest that in their view (to turn Orwell somewhat on his head) some Russians may not be as Russian as others.[36]

Putin is not alone, and many others are far less circumspect. Ethnically biased statements by political and opinion leaders are not uncommon, and those who voice them are rarely taken to task.[37] Human rights activists speak of a "wave of racism" "gathering force" in Russia and cite the beatings of blacks, Hindus, and Caucasians in Moscow.[38] The Council of Europe's European Commission Against Racism and Intolerance's November 2001 study reported official discrimination against ethnic and religious minorities in Russia at all levels. Antisemitic violence and the use of "extreme nationalist, racist, and xenophobic propaganda" by political parties and the media and violence against minority people were discussed in this report.[39] Certainly anecdotal reports abound of street violence targeted at Jews, Caucasians, Africans, and other minorities, especially in large cities such as Moscow and St. Petersburg, although many officials deny the problem is widespread.[40] Recent antisemitic attacks have included a booby-trapped sign on the side of the road that

---

[36]Astrid Tuminez, "Russian Nationalism and Vladimir Putin's Russia," PONARS, 2000.

[37]Deputies to Russia's parliament, the Duma, have openly made antisemitic remarks, as did Krasnodar province Governor Nikolai Kondratenko. Human Rights Watch has accused Moscow Mayor Yuri Luzhkov of "silently endorsing" police violence against ethnic minorities. See Human Rights Watch, *World Report 1999* and *World Report 2000*.

[38]"Human Rights Activists Condemn 'Wave of Racism in Russia,'" *RFE/RL Newsline*, Vol. 5, No. 217, Part I, November 15, 2001.

[39]"Council of Europe Says Racism Widespread in Russia," *RFE/RL Newsline*, Vol. 5, No. 216, Part I, November 14, 2001.

[40]John Daniszewski, "Racism Rears Up in Russia," *Los Angeles Times*, June 14, 2001.

injured a woman in June 2002 and a variety of regional attacks on individuals.[41]

Ethnic discord is also reflected in polls of military personnel. Mono-ethnic units are increasingly common as are ethnic cliques (although regional cliques are even more common). Thirty percent of soldiers polled say they dislike individuals of one or another ethnic group.[42] On the other hand, some recent survey research suggests that familiarity breeds at least a measure of tolerance—Russians who grow up in predominantly Muslim or Buddhist republics tend to be more tolerant of other faiths.[43]

The more disturbing side of Russian attitudes, however, may be reflected in an article published by the popular *Literaturnaya Gazeta* in May 2001 that argued that negative views of people of Caucasian background are a result of bad behavior by Caucasians and their lack of respect for Russian customs and women.[44] Similarly, a journalist in an Armenian newspaper wrote in January 2002 that the un-"guest"-like behavior of Caucasians in Russia, as well as their criminal activities, leads to ill feeling among Russians toward those with darker skin and Caucasian features.[45]

The ethnic question takes on a particularly interesting dimension in the Far East. During late Soviet times, this region enjoyed a steady influx of Russians who received significant subsidies to relocate to this rather inhospitable area (before that, it was a popular location for prison camps). With the collapse of the USSR, these subsidies came to an end and the cost of living in these regions increased drastically. It became increasingly expensive to deliver food and supplies to the Far East. Poverty increased even as the region began to face

---

[41]Sabrina Tavernise, "Bomb Attack Shows that Russia Hasn't Rooted Out Anti-Semitism," *New York Times*, June 1, 2002.

[42]"Ethnic Conflicts Increase in Russian Army," *RFE/RL Newsline*, Vol. 5, No. 163, Part I, August 28, 2001.

[43]Susan Goodrich Lehman, "Inter-Ethnic Conflict in the Republics of Russia in Light of Religious Revival," *Post-Soviet Geography and Economics*, Vol. 39, No. 8, 1998.

[44]"Negative Attitudes Toward People from the Caucasus Defended," *RFE/RL Newsline*, Vol. 5, No. 112, Part I, June 13, 2001.

[45]Rouben Ayrapetyan, "Ill Treatment of Caucasians in Russia Rooted in Behaviour—Armenian Analyst," *Johnson's Russia List* (BBC Monitoring, Azg), January 9, 2002.

heat and energy shortages and cutoffs. As a result, increasing numbers of residents of this region sought to move west, to European
Russia.[46] There have been severe population drops in the region,
even as those who remain continue to face hardship. Many in Russia
see this as a dangerous development. In August 2001, a State Council
Working Group prepared a concept paper on Siberian and Far
Eastern development recommending that the Russian government
take steps to maintain the population in the Far East and promote its
growth.[47] A resumption of the subsidies and fringe benefits that ac-
crued to residents of this region seems highly unlikely, given resource constraints.

At the same time as Russians have begun to leave the Far East, increasing numbers of Chinese citizens have, over the past ten years,
begun crossing the border from the People's Republic. For the most
part, they do not come to stay, but rather to engage in business,
make some money, and return home. They may do this repeatedly,
although a few do take up residence more permanently. What is
most significant is not the numbers of Chinese entering Russia
(which Russian sources estimate to be only in the tens of thousands),
but the overwhelmingly negative attitude of local Russians to these
immigrants. Numerous articles in the Russian press refer to the
Chinese immigration as an "invasion," and Russian officials have
even dubbed the influx of illegal immigrants a security threat.

Research by Mikhail Alexseev suggests that fears of Chinese demographic encroachment in the Far East are far more a matter of perception than reality, although as perceptions go, this one has its
potential dangers. His research in Primorsky Krai, where Chinese migrants are no more than 1.5 percent of the local population, suggests
that local Russians tend to overestimate the Chinese proportion of
the population by a very large factor, with 46 percent of survey respondents estimating it at 10–20 percent. They also expect this situation to get "worse" with rapid growth of the Chinese population

---

[46]Gerber, "Russia's Population Crisis: The Migration Dimension."

[47]"Moscow Plans to Try to Hold Russian Population in Siberia," *RFE/RL Newsline*, Vol.
5, No. 164, Part I, August 29, 2001.

relative to that of the Russian population. Moreover, most respondents described Chinese migrants as a threat to their region.[48]

Alexseev found that most Primorsky Krai residents surveyed expect an eventual Chinese annexation of the region, perhaps on historical grounds, although they think this will happen peacefully, perhaps by means of a willing Russian handover of the territory or perhaps just by means of demographic preponderance, something Alexseev terms an "ethnic security dilemma." Most of those surveyed are opposed to Russian-Chinese intermarriage and many support a ban on Chinese citizens entering Primorsky Krai to trade.[49]

Thus, while the ethnic situation in Russia as a whole creates grounds for concern, that in the Far East suggests the potential for conflict that could involve another nuclear-armed state—perhaps if harassment or ill-treatment of Chinese immigrants or migrants spurs Beijing to take action. That said, the professed desire of Russian officials to build a civic society based on nationalism, not ethnicity, provides grounds for some optimism. The anecdotal reports of racist violence, racist statements by politicians and officials, and the acceptance of racist attitudes such as found in the *Literaturnaya Gazeta* piece mentioned above do suggest the potential for ethnic cleavage. Insofar as ethnicity and region are correlated, and both of these coincide with economic disparities, the potential for ethno-regional political mobilization also increases. But it does not mean that ethnic conflict will necessarily or even probably emerge, just that the potential exists and the situation bears watching. Of particular interest are government responses to racist actions and statements, including those by officials themselves, and the evolving attitudes in the Far East.

---

[48]Mikhail Alexseev, "The Chinese Are Coming: Public Opinion and Threat Perception in the Russian Far East," PONARS, 2001.

[49]Ibid.

Chapter Six

THE RUSSIAN MILITARY

PUTIN AND THE MILITARY

Vladimir Putin has taken pains to court the military, both as an electoral bloc and as a political force. When he took power in early 2000, he promised higher defense spending, including higher salaries.[1] His handling of the second Chechnya war met with considerable favor in military circles, which saw the president as giving the armed forces a freer hand. This seemed a positive development given the rising belief among Russian military personnel (and others) that the first war was "lost" because civilians insisted on a peace treaty—whereas the military could have won given enough time (the situation on the ground in Chechnya in late summer 1996 suggests otherwise).[2] Brian Taylor writes that Putin's promises, combined with his general attitude of pride and effusiveness when talking about the military, increased morale as well as support for the new president.[3]

Relations between the president and the armed forces have deteriorated since that time (as Taylor predicted).[4] The promised pay raises came to be seen by many as too little, too late, particularly as they do

---

[1]Brian Taylor, "Putin and the Military: How Long Will the Honeymoon Last?" PONARS, 2000.

[2]Olga Oliker, *Russia's Chechen Wars: Lessons from Urban Combat*, RAND, MR-1289-A, 2001, pp. 30–31, 34–36; Taylor, "Putin and the Military: How Long Will the Honeymoon Last?"

[3]Taylor, "Putin and the Military: How Long Will the Honeymoon Last?"

[4]Ibid.

not appear to be forthcoming. More recently, the post–September 11 rapprochement with the United States, acceptance of the U.S. decision to withdraw from the Antiballistic Missile (ABM) treaty, and the closing of bases in Vietnam and Cuba have led to increased distrust of the president among many military personnel.[5]

Today, most analysts agree that military personnel are largely absent from Putin's inner circle.[6] Continued disagreement between the Minister of Defense and his staff and the General Staff chief over issues of general and specific strategy, which became very public in 2000 (when Igor' Sergeev was defense minister), remains a factor, especially given rumors that current Defense Minister Sergei Ivanov initially sought to oust General Staff Chief Anatoly Kvashnin.[7] Putin presumably appointed FSB veteran and former National Security Council chief Ivanov to the post of defense minister in part to have a trusted colleague in that job, and Ivanov has, in turn, surrounded himself with his own trusted staff and replaced or shifted around a number of top-ranked generals.[8] In recent months, however, reports that the president is increasingly reliant on Kvashnin for briefings and recommendations on the situation in Afghanistan and the war on terrorism more generally, while Ivanov has shifted to the background, suggest the possibility that Kvashnin's influence may be on the rise.[9]

Putin has transferred overall authority for the Chechnya campaign to the FSB, although reportedly military commanders remain very

---

[5]Igor' Korotchenko, "Army leadership under FSB oversight," *Nezavisimoye Voyennoye Obozreniye*, December 7, 2001; Vadim Solovyov, "Military commanders increase pressure on Kremlin," *Nezavisimoye Voyennoye Obozreniye*, November 16, 2001.

[6]Pavel Baev, "Putin's Court: How the Military Fits In," PONARS, 2000; Solovyov, "Military commanders increase pressure on Kremlin."

[7]Baev, "Putin's Court: How the Military Fits In;" Korotchenko, "Army leadership under FSB oversight."

[8]Pavel Baev, "President Putin and His Generals: Bureaucratic Control and War-Fighting Culture," PONARS, 2001; Vadim Solovyov, "Glorification in the service of a single political-military leadership," *Nezavisimoye Voyennoye Obozreniye*, November 30, 2001.

[9]Baev, "Putin's Court: How the Military Fits In"; Korotchenko, "Army leadership under FSB oversight"; Solovyov, "Military commanders increase pressure on Kremlin."

much in control on the ground.[10] Putin is also said to rely on the FSB for information about developments in the armed forces. The military Counterintelligence Directorate, which has personnel throughout the Russian military, reports to the FSB, reportedly on everything from goings-on at the platoon level to those at the office of the defense minister.[11]

That said, the military continues to enjoy fairly independent decisionmaking. Baev writes that as long as Putin is committed to a military settlement of the situation in Chechnya, he needs the military on his side and will therefore remain willing to compromise—although he is unwilling to commit to the levels of wholesale destruction that some military planners may advocate. Baev believes that Putin fears the rise of military influence, particularly that of the generals now in charge of the Chechnya campaign.[12] Some argue that it was the military leaders' hard-line position that precluded compromise by the Russian government on the ABM treaty, leading eventually to U.S. withdrawal from the treaty.[13]

The military is relatively unencumbered by interference from the legislature. The Duma has no authority over the Defense Ministry (or any other executive branch) appointments and has no real transparency into the military budget, which remains highly opaque with just a few very general line items accounting for most of the funds. The Ministries of Finance and Defense take advantage of these to shift funds between programs.[14] If anything, the budget has grown even less transparent recently, with the disappearance of information about the extent to which military procurement orders have

---

[10]Baev, "President Putin and His Generals: Bureaucratic Control and War-Fighting Culture."

[11]Korotchenko, "Army leadership under FSB oversight."

[12]Baev, "President Putin and His Generals: Bureaucratic Control and War-Fighting Culture."

[13]Solovyov, "Military commanders increase pressure on Kremlin."

[14]Brian Taylor, "The Duma and Military Reform," PONARS, 2000.

been fulfilled.[15] The MVD forces, which are not included in the military budget, are under even less oversight.[16]

The Duma has sought to establish legislation to increase its oversight of the armed services. One example is the largely ignored 1998 law on budget classification, which would prohibit the vague line items that make up the military budget. However, they have had little success to date.[17] Conversely, there is an increasing sense within the military that the Duma can be an effective ally against the administration, especially in efforts to increase the defense budget: more military officers have recently been providing testimony to Duma committees on a range of issues.[18]

MILITARY REGIONALIZATION

Federal funding shortfalls, wage arrears to soldiers, and difficulties supplying military forces in the provinces have led to a devolution of some of these missions to the local level. During the 1990s, authorities in several Russian regions took on the responsibility for paying, feeding, and housing soldiers based on their territory. In many cases, other services were also arranged with local governments. Some military units supplemented whatever federal or local monies they received by engaging in independent entrepreneurship, such as bartering the use of military transport vehicles or soldiers' labor for food.[19]

---

[15]Vadim Solovyov, "Government proposes one-third increase in military budget," *Nezavisimoye Voyennoye Obozreniye*, September 7, 2001.

[16]Viktor Ozerov, "Point of view: Whose finger should be on the pulse?" *Armeiskii Sbornik*, No. 3, March 2001. Although some argue that the MVD, FSB, and other power ministries (i.e., those who command troops) receive funding that might be better allocated to the MoD, Taylor argues that this has been overstated, and that, moreover, Putin's FSB background will preclude any significant cuts to the funding of it or its sister organizations. (Taylor, "Putin and the Military: How Long Will the Honeymoon Last?")

[17]Taylor, "The Duma and Military Reform."

[18]Ibid.

[19]Bruce Blair and Clifford G. Gaddy, "Russia's Aging War Machine," *Brookings Review*, Summer 1999.

The result was increasing economic dependence on regional governments, who often provided supplies with charge. Examples include the payment of wage arrears to Pacific Fleet sailors by Governor Viktor Nazdratenko and suggestions by Krasnoyarsk Governor Lebed' that he would take similar steps.[20] According to Nikolai Sokov, commanders in the Siberian Military District say that they receive most of their support from regional governments and are careful to get local officials' approval for military activities. The Strategic Rocket Forces unit based in Orenburg Krai was sufficiently grateful to regional officials for providing housing, food, funds for training, and other necessities that its command has sought to have the unit officially renamed "Orenburgskaya." A similar dependency on local support reportedly exists in Saratov, where Russia's newest Topol-M (SS-27) missiles are deployed.[21]

One of the concessions regional officials have received in exchange for their support of military forces is that conscripts are now generally allowed to fulfill their service requirements near their homes (unlike officers, who are rotated in and out of duty locations). This was the deal negotiated by Nazdratenko for the Pacific Fleet and by a range of other leaders for their regions.[22] In line with this, many regional governments now fully support the call-up and conscription process in their areas.[23]

These relationships, which Treisman argues were cultivated on a personal level by regional leaders during the 1990s, and which Herd describes as "de facto alliances between local military commanders and regional political elites," are seen by many as a dangerous example of regionalization, one that calls into question the loyalty of soldiers to Russia itself if they are called upon to fight.[24] Sokov takes a somewhat different perspective, suggesting that these partnerships

---

[20]Herd, "Russia: Systemic Transformation or Federal Collapse?"

[21]Nikolai Sokov, "The Reality and Myths of Nuclear Regionalism in Russia," PONARS, 2000.

[22]Herd, "Russia: Systemic Transformation or Federal Collapse?"; Treisman, *After the Deluge: Regional Crises and Political Consolidation in Russia.*

[23]Sokov, "The Reality and Myths of Nuclear Regionalism in Russia"; Herd, "Russia: Systemic Transformation or Federal Collapse?"

[24]Treisman, *After the Deluge: Regional Crises and Political Consolidation in Russia,* pp. 14–15.

are fairly pragmatic in nature. Local regional leaders are not seeking their own military forces, but rather leverage in their dealings with the federal government (as well as electoral support from the military and their families). The military (and, according to Sokov, particularly Military District commanders) similarly gains an important ally. By coordinating policy and approaches, both groups gain needed support. Aside from the much-needed supplies, Sokov notes that military forces have benefited in quarrels with energy providers, which have recently sought to shut off power to bases in Altai and Khabarovsk as a result of nonpayment. When military units took control of energy-supply facilities to restore power, local leaders intervened on the military's behalf.[25]

One can also argue that the Chechnya experience demonstrates that Russian soldiers, conscript and professional, will serve when called upon, and will fight, even within Russian borders. Even if increasing military regionalization is one more sign of Moscow's uncertain control of the country, the phenomenon is unlikely to lead to crisis in the foreseeable future. Russian military affairs specialist Dmitri Trenin argues, for example, that it is highly improbable that Ministry of Defense (or MVD) armed forces personnel would support a local effort to secede, for it is the professional officers who continue to run the military organizations and their loyalty is to Moscow. However, he also argues that in the unlikely event of regional secession, troops may be unwilling to repeat the experience of Chechnya and fire on their countrymen, armed or otherwise. Even in Chechnya, where years of interethnic hatred spurred strong anti-Chechen feeling on the part of Russian troops, members of the Russian military repeatedly expressed distaste at being used as an internal police force, a mission they see as incommensurate with their training and duties.

This opposition to an internal security role has roots both in the nature of professional militaries as well as in the particular events and organizational incentives that have occurred in Russia in the past decade. In 1991 and 1993, officers who maintained that the military's role was only to protect the state from external threats won this debate and were rewarded with positions of power both within the general staff and in the Ministry of Defense for their support of the

---

[25]Sokov, "The Reality and Myths of Nuclear Regionalism in Russia."

Yeltsin regime and their nonparticipation in the putsch attempt. This process effectively marginalized anyone who disagreed and isolated them from positions of command.[26]

CONVENTIONAL FORCES: PERSONNEL AND EQUIPMENT

Indicators of the current state of Russian conventional forces are confusing at best, self-contradictory at worst. The Soviet experience in Afghanistan, followed by Russia's 1994–1996 fight for sovereignty over Chechnya, suggested a force in disrepair, with poorly supplied, untrained soldiers and a largely incompetent command. But the Russian army's performance in its return to Chechnya in 1999 (which continues at the time of this writing) demonstrates a significantly more capable military, with improved planning and implementation, functioning command and control, and the very real ability to wage and win a local war.[27]

In fact, the Russian military today represents both that seen in Chechnya 1994 and in Chechnya 1999. Russia can wage a local war effectively, but only by calling upon its most capable units from throughout its armed forces to cobble together a force. Even then, it favors an approach to military operations that relies on destructive capability over skill or precision, sometimes to the detriment of combat (to say nothing of political) aims.[28] As Taylor aptly notes, "the Russian armed forces insist on maintaining a first-world military on a third-world budget." With numerous "power ministries" such as the MVD fielding their own heavily armed forces, Russia has more people under arms than does the United States—with a much smaller economy. As a result, Russia spends some $4000 per soldier per year whereas the United States spends 45 times that on each soldier (and Turkey spends over three times the Russian allocation).[29]

---

[26]Tanya Charlick-Paley, "Accommodating to the Loss of Empire: Is There a Post-Imperial Military Syndrome?" Ph.D. Dissertation, Ohio State University, 1997, pp. 170–175; and author discussion with Dmitri Trenin, June 21, 2000.

[27]For a comparison of Russian capability and fighting in the two wars with a focus on urban combat, see Oliker, *Russia's Chechen Wars.*

[28]Ibid.

[29]Taylor, "Putin and the Military: How Long Will the Honeymoon Last?"

The challenges faced by the Russian armed forces today begin with the young men who are drafted into the military each year, one-third or more of whom (40 percent in 2001) are deemed ineligible for health reasons.[30] Of those who do serve, over half have some sort of medical restriction on their service. While these figures may be somewhat exaggerated by the large numbers of young Russian men who seek falsified medical waivers to avoid the draft, there is no question that the health crisis has had a significant effect on military conscription. And even the healthy may not remain so once inducted. The military health service is no improvement over that in the civilian sector, where shortages of supplies and medicines are rampant. Moreover, the impact of narcotics abuse in Russia's military is aptly illustrated by tales of soldiers in Chechnya who traded weapons to the enemy in exchange for drugs.[31]   Hazing, or *dedovshchina*—the systematic harassment, rape, and torture of young recruits by older soldiers—continues to be prevalent. Authorities turn a blind eye while hundreds of young Russian men die each year (some directly as a result of injuries from beatings; others indirectly through suicide).[32] *Dedovshchina* remains a problem even in combat: a soldier interviewed in a military hospital early in 2000 had survived the bloody 1999–2000 battle of Grozny unscathed. It was a beating from his comrades that had caused him to be hospitalized.[33]

Educational levels for conscripts have dropped, and the increasing prevalence of crime in society is reflected in the military as well. Half of conscripts willingly report some contact with illegal activity and 8 percent of those called up have criminal records. Unless the conviction was for a particularly serious offense, such as murder, a record does not preclude service in Russia. As of early 1998, more than 20,000 of the 1.4 million people serving in Russia's armed forces had a criminal past, with convictions ranging from hooliganism to rob-

---

[30]Nail' Gaftulin, "Yet another crisis"; Brantsen, "Russia: Poor Fitness of Conscripts Points to Public Health Crisis."

[31]Aleksandr Sinitzin, "In Mozdok they drink to life" (in Russian), Vesti.ru, January 27, 2000, http://vesti.ru/daynews/2000/01.27/15chechnya/.

[32]Mark Galeotti, "Russia's Criminal Army," *Jane's Intelligence Review,* Vol. 11, No. 6, June 1999, pp. 8–10.

[33]Sergei Krapivin, "War does not have a 'parade' face" (in Russian), *Vecherniy Cheliabinsk,* January 28, 2000.

bery. In today's force, 40 percent of conscripts are deemed by their commanders to be insufficiently trustworthy to lead. An equal number is precluded from access to strategically important assets or information.[34]

Transitioning from a conscription-based system to an all-volunteer force has been a much discussed reform possibility for many years. However, the current rate of retention of contract soldiers for a year or more is less than 20 percent.[35] To attract and retain quality people, comprehensive changes would have to be made in Russia's system of training, equipping, and paying its soldiers, to make the military an attractive career for more young men and women.

Moreover, it is clear that the military's problems are not limited to conscripts. Crime and corruption at a variety of levels are evidenced by the multiple cases of illegal sales of military hardware that have come to light since the end of the Cold War. These include the "fire sale" of individual weapons by Soviet/Russian forces stationed and then withdrawn from Eastern Europe in the late 1980s and early 1990s, as well as what is reportedly a significant underground market in heavy equipment, perhaps even armored vehicles and fighter aircraft. Arrests and prosecutions of military personnel for such actions confirm that they continue. Russian officers and men deployed to international peacekeeping operations, including in the former Yugoslavia, have sold everything from weapons parts to fuel on local black markets.[36]

Such illegal activities continued even under fire in Chechnya. As already noted, tales of Russian forces trading ammunition to the enemy in exchange for narcotics were numerous, as were those of rebel

---

[34]Vladimir Ermolin, "An army of shooting drug addicts" (in Russian), *Russkii Telegraf*, January 28, 1998, No. 12(84); Aleksandr Yankov, Igor' Zadorozhniy, and Vadim Vinnik, "Prevention of 'barracks crime'" (in Russian), *Armeiskii Sbornik*, March 2000; Vladimir Mukhin, "Every other youth has never studied anywhere" (in Russian), *Nezavisimaya Gazeta*, April 5, 2000, No. 61 (2123), Internet edition, nvo.ng.ru/events/2000-04-05/2_yuth.html.

[35]Solovyov, "Government proposes one-third increase in military budget."

[36]See Graham H. Turbiville, Jr., *Mafia in Uniform: The Criminalization of the Russian Armed Forces*, Foreign Military Studies Office, Fort Leavenworth, Kansas, 1995, www.call.army.mil/call/fmso/fmsopubs/issues/mafia.htm; Galeotti, "Russia's Criminal Army."

forces paying off Russian artillery troops not to fire.[37] In an area with a rampant illegal slave trade, there were even reports of officers and noncommissioned officers (NCOs) selling their men into slavery.[38]

The Chechen campaigns pointed up shortfalls in training, force co-ordination, and the deterioration of Russian military equipment. Although the second war showed marked improvement in the first two categories, this resulted in large part from intensive and targeted preparation during the interwar period for specific tasks (such as mountain combat) and for coordination between disparate forces. A concerted effort to minimize the use of conscripts and to send only trained forces into combat was also a factor. A decision to focus on creating a small number of higher-readiness units contributed to Russia's ability to fight this war. However, lack of training in urban combat led to severe casualties, and, despite real improvement, there were myriad force coordination problems both between different power ministries (for example, Ministry of Defense and MVD troops) and between different kinds of forces (air and ground).[39]

The second Chechen war has demonstrated conclusively that Russia can successfully and effectively deploy and supply a sizable force in a local conflict. This is important, but it must be understood in con-text. Baev writes that what few high-readiness divisions the Russian army has are currently either rotating between Chechnya and the Balkans or deployed near Moscow—there are insufficient competent forces to meet much in the way of other commitments, should those arise.[40] The state of Russia's military equipment is equally trouble-some. Russia's military industrial complex, once perceived world-wide as a powerful entity, has been particularly hard hit over the last ten years. It has been unable to equip its soldiers with state-of-the-art equipment or to effectively maintain existing systems. The

---

[37]Sinitzin, "In Mozdok they drink to life"; Bakhtiyar Ahmedakhanov, "Soldiers bargaining with own death" (in Russian), *Obshchaya Gazeta*, February 17, 2000, Internet edition, www.og.ru/mat/rep2.shtml.

[38]Aleksandr Egorenko, "Betrayed and sold" (in Russian), *Izvestiya*, No. 200, October 23, 1999, p. 5.

[39]Oliker, *Russia's Chechen Wars*, pp. 36–38, 51, 54, 57.

[40]Baev, "President Putin and His Generals: Bureaucratic Control and War-Fighting Culture."

diminished capacity to build new weaponry, combined with Russia's inability to pay for it and, despite significant efforts, the relative paucity of orders from abroad given the loss of the East European market, make the sustainability of the weapons complex questionable.[41]

Russian aircraft and other systems are increasingly out of date and lack many modern components, such as night-vision capability.[42] Some argue that even before they began to age, these systems were inferior to U.S.-built weaponry, required far more frequent repairs, and lasted at best half as long. Russian tanks are highly vulnerable to foreign antitank capabilities, which are developing more quickly than are Russian defensive systems. Russian precision weapons are dependent on laser sights that can be easily defeated by smoke-screens (and can reveal the location of Russian forces).[43] Reports indicate that even new systems are problematical: according to Mikhail Rastopshin, Russia's new antitank weapons are only some 50 percent effective against the reactive armor that is standard on many potential adversary tanks.[44]

Fuel shortages and the poor condition of equipment have shrunk the ability to exercise and train. Fuel and ammunition shortages preclude live-fire exercises at anything near the frequency that is needed to maintain competence. The August 2000 naval exercises that will remain forever infamous for the sinking of the Kursk sub-marine demonstrated the extreme deterioration of naval capability and training even if the Kursk tragedy is left out of the analysis.[45] Sources vary on the average annual number of flight hours for Russian pilots (from 12 to 25 or so), but they are clearly far lower than

---

[41]Mikhail Rastopshin, "In old wineskins even new wine will soon go sour," *Nezavisimoye Voyennoye Obozreniye*, August 10, 2001; Aleksandr Simonenko and Roman Tovstik, "Ordered to survive," *Armeiskii Sbornik*, No. 10, October 2001.

[42]Sergei Sokut, "Making sense of the Chechen experience," *Nezavisimoye Voyennoye Obozreniye*, August 10, 2001.

[43]Rastopshin, "In old wineskins even new wine will soon go sour."

[44]Mikhail Rastopshin, "From an armaments program to a disarmament program," *Nezavisimoye Voyennoye Obozreniye*, January 19, 2002.

[45]Yuri Klyuev, "Military naval exercises: How it's done," *Izvestia*, December 3, 2001.

the hundreds of training hours Western pilots spend in the air.[46] Moreover, with junior pilots receiving far less training, the most qualified pilots are aging rapidly; the average age of Russia's top pilots is now 41–43 years (in a system with a mandatory retirement age of 45).[47]

The impact on Russian military capability was evident in Chechnya. Russian ground forces, helicopters, and most airplanes lacked night-vision capability (the equipment, the skills, or both). Shortages of serviceable rotary and fixed-wing aircraft led to repeated patching and repairs of deployed assets in the field, well beyond the point when the aircraft were safe to operate; replacements were simply unavailable.[48]

The experience of the Chechen war combined with the diminished capacity of the military-industrial complex has reportedly led the Russian military to adopt a new focus on systems modernization. Reports indicate that first priority be on troops geared for limited conflict, with later attention to strategic assets. For air power, this translates into modernization first for army and tactical aviation, then for transport aircraft, and finally for strategic aircraft. The modernization plan projects having 20–25 percent of aircraft at a fourth-generation-plus level by 2005. The funding focus is on approaches that can be applied at low cost and across platforms. Night vision for helicopters and planes is a clear priority.[49]

As Mikhail Rastopshin notes, however, there is a limit to how much can be attained by modernizing aging systems. As he points out, mounting new antitank guided missiles (ATGMs) on old helicopters will only lead to the destruction of the new weaponry if the helicopters are shot down. Although new systems exist on the drawing board, and some are even in prototype, there is little expectation that

---

[46]Blair and Gaddy, "Russia's Aging War Machine"; Simonenko and Tovstik, "Ordered to survive"; Sergei Sokut, "Perspectives for the development of combat aviation," *Nezavisimoye Voyennoye Obozreniye*, August 10, 2001.

[47]Viktor Kozlov, "Point of view: Don't joke with airpower," *Armeiskii Sbornik*, No. 10, October 2001; "Russian Air Force in Trouble," *RFE/RL Newsline*, Vol. 5, No. 111, Part I, June 12, 2001.

[48]Oliker, *Russia's Chechen Wars*, p. 57.

[49]Sokut, "Making sense of the Chechen experience."

any new aircraft, armor, or ships will enter into service before 2010.[50] Thus, while much is written about Russian plans for new fighter aircraft, transport planes, unmanned systems, and satellites, the extent to which these plans will transform into real weapon systems remains questionable.

Russia's newly announced armaments program through 2002 should be seen in this context. Although it promises two new types of helicopters and a fifth-generation aircraft as well as continued modernization of existing systems, it seems questionable that the promised "100 percent" supply of the army and navy with arms and equipment and various increases in combat potential (20 percent improvement is promised for the missile complex, 15 percent for the air force, and 30 percent for warships, etc.) can be attained.[51]

There is no question that comprehensive reform is needed for the Russian military to survive, much less succeed. But although the Russian military has shrunk from the force inherited from the USSR, reform itself has been elusive. What remains is instead a smaller, much deteriorated variation on the Soviet military. Plans for reform are plentiful. Vladimir Putin, for instance, has said that he plans to transition the armed forces to be "compact, mobile, and modernized." But neither the plans nor the money for such an endeavor appears to be forthcoming. As Pavel Baev points out, Russia's published material on its national security concept and military doctrine is largely silent on the question of military reform.[52]

Comprehensive reform has few fans among members of the armed services, who fear the loss of their jobs and associated fringe benefits, such as housing.[53] In early November 2001, an open letter to the president and government signed by retired senior military officers with continued close links to serving senior officers of the General

---

[50]Rastopshin, "From an armaments program to a disarmament program"; Rastopshin, "In old wineskins even new wine will soon go sour."

[51]"Defense Ministry Official Outlines Russia's Arms Program Up to 2010," ITAR-TASS, 1822 GMT, January 29, 2002; Rastopshin, "From an armaments program to a disarmament program."

[52]Baev, "Putin's Court: How the Military Fits In."

[53]Ibid.

Staff described ongoing reforms in Russia, including military reform, as "reforms of death" and called for the return of rule to the people.[54]

The letter-writers' fears aside, little has in fact been accomplished in military reform since Vladimir Putin took office. Although Minister of Defense Sergei Ivanov spoke in favor of sharp cuts in the military forces (although not non-MoD forces) when he was Security Council chief, his tenure as minister has not led to comprehensive changes (although he has recently said that Russian military forces will shrink by nearly 100,000 men in 2002 and 260,000–270,000 more in the years after[55]).[56] In November 2001, Putin met with the military leadership to outline four directions for military policy in the coming year: (1) reassessment of priorities, particularly to coordinate with other members of the counter-terror coalition; (2) identification of priorities for military development and reallocation of resources accordingly; (3) optimization of the structure of the armed forces, to include improvements in preparedness; and (4) social support.[57] None of these concepts is new, of course, and, without a comprehensive strategy of how to attain, for example, an optimized force structure or pay for social support, none of them appears particularly meaningful. Organizational changes, such as the recreation of the Ground Forces Command in March 2001 (the command was disbanded in 1997, at which time ground forces units in coastal areas were made subordinate to the navy), plans to transition to a "three-service structure" (ground, naval, and air), and the adoption of a new naval doctrine in 2001 (which appears to create a sort of Ministry of the Navy), have as yet had limited apparent impact.[58]

Planning numbers may provide more insight. The goal once expressed by former President Yeltsin—that 3.5 percent of the federal budget should be spent on the military—has yet to be attained. The

---

[54]Solovyov, "Military commanders increase pressure on Kremlin."

[55]Solovyov, "Government proposes one-third increase in military budget."

[56]Taylor, "The Duma and Military Reform."

[57]Solovyov, "Military commanders increase pressure on Kremlin."

[58]Baev, "President Putin and His Generals: Bureaucratic Control and War-Fighting Culture"; Mikhail Khodarenok, "Does Russia need air-space defense," *Nezavisimoye Voyennoye Obozreniye*, September 7, 2001; Vadim Solovyov, "Russia has acquired yet another doctrine—naval," *Nezavisimoye Voyennoye Obozreniye*, August 3, 2001.

2.77 percent allocated to the military budget in 2001 has dropped to 2.5 percent in 2002. Although the budget has grown in terms of sheer numbers (284.18 billion rubles, or approximately $9 billion for 2002), inflation mitigates this increase considerably. That said, the allocation of the budget, which as of 2002 shifts considerably more funds to procurement (an increase of nearly 40 percent), may reflect changing priorities.[59]

NUCLEAR STRATEGY AND FORCES

Russia's current published military doctrine does not preclude the use of nuclear weapons as a last resort, even if the other side has not used, and has shown no intention of using, nuclear weapons. This is not in and of itself cause for panic: U.S. policy on the use of nuclear weapons is quite similar in eschewing a "no first use" pledge. That said, a conventionally weakened Russia would doubtless exhaust its nonnuclear alternatives far more quickly than would the militarily capable United States. If a local war in Chechnya proved a serious challenge for Russia's conventional forces, a genuine interstate conflict against a more capable foe could create real dangers of triggering nuclear weapon employment.

This situation has not escaped Russian planners. The pages of military journals over the last few years have been full of debate as to the appropriateness of, and strategy and tactics for, nuclear weapons employment. Advocates of an increased focus on nuclear weapons emphasize Russia's conventional weakness, particularly in precision weapons, and economic circumstances. They argue that nuclear weapons are an ideal deterrent for Russia against any sort of attack, being an existent, well-known technology and cheap compared with conventional weapons improvements. Within this approach, one school of thought looks at the deterrence aspects of nuclear weapons, arguing that nuclear deterrence should be the foundation of Russian military strategy, although nuclear weapons would not be used militarily.[60] Others favor a doctrine in which nuclear weapons

---

[59]Lyuba Pronina, "State OKs $2.5 Bln Arms Budget," *Moscow Times*, January 18, 2002; Solovyov, "Government proposes one-third increase in military budget."

[60]Stanislav Voronin and Sergei Brezkun, "Strategically beneficial asymmetry," *Nezavisimoye Voyennoye Obozreniye*, September 18, 1999.

are seen as somewhat more "usable," an approach described as nuclear "de-escalation." In the event of an attack on the Russian Federation, a limited nuclear strike (with tactical or "operational" nuclear weapons) would communicate Russia's resolve to the aggressor and thus lead it to step down its attack. If this fails, further "de-escalative" strikes on a ladder of escalation are launched, until the aggressor stands down or a large-scale nuclear exchange ensues (at which point de-escalation can be assumed to have failed).[61]

The de-escalation approach appears to have been incorporated to some extent into the Zapad-99 military exercise (June 1999). The scenario for this exercise involved an attack on Russia and Belarus by a "Blue" force highly reminiscent of the NATO force involved in the Yugoslavia campaign. When joint Russian-Belarusan conventional efforts are insufficient to stop the attack, Russia carries out limited nuclear strikes, described as "preventive," on enemy territory.[62]

Shortly after the Zapad-99 exercise, then-President Yeltsin dismissed the notion of large-scale aggression against Russia as science fiction.[63] Nonetheless, David Yost writes that several additional exercises also focused on nuclear use, simulating the launch of nuclear missiles from heavy and medium bombers.[64] Kipp, however, argues that the combination of NATO's campaign in Yugoslavia and then–Defense Minister Sergeev's disappointment with the Zapad-99 exercises led to a decision that nuclear weapons would be viewed primarily in their deterrence capacity and that Russia would need to develop more advanced conventional weapons for local and smaller-

---

[61]See Jacob W. Kipp, "Russia's Nonstrategic Nuclear Weapons," *Military Review,* May–June 2001; V. I. Levshin, A. V. Nedelin, and Mikhail Sosnovskiy, "Use of nuclear weapons to de-escalate military operations," *Voennaia Mysl,* No. 3, May–June 1999; Vladimir Sivolov and Mikhail Sosnovskiy, "Reality of deterrence," *Nezavisimoye Voyennoye Obozreniye,* October 22, 1999; David S. Yost, "Russia's Non-Strategic Nuclear Forces," *International Affairs,* Vol. 77, No. 3, 2001.

[62]On the Zapad-99 exercise, see Vladimir Georgiev, "Two weeks ago Russia used nuclear weapons," *Emerging Markets Database (Nezavisimaya Gazeta),* July 14, 1999; Yuri Golotyuk, "Defense Ministry Premiere on 'Western Theater,'" *Emerging Markets (Izvestia),* June 29, 1999; Aleksandr Gol'tz, "A different war," *Emerging Markets Database (Itogi),* August 3, 1999; Igor' Korotchenko, "Russian army prepares to defeat aggression," *Emerging Markets Database (Nezavisimaya Gazeta),* June 23, 1999.

[63]Kipp, "Russia's Nonstrategic Nuclear Weapons."

[64]Yost, "Russia's Non-Strategic Nuclear Forces."

scale conflict contingencies (although nonstrategic nuclear weapons might still play a deterrence role in local wars as well). However, until advanced systems are developed and fielded, Kipp believes that Russia will continue to rely on nuclear weapons in the near term, lowering the threshold for nuclear use.[65] The evidence of more recent large-scale exercises, such as Combat Brotherhood 2001, which, although still positing a potential NATO or NATO-like enemy, have not involved nuclear weapons use,[66] suggests that de-escalation may be off the table for the time being. While the true extent to which it or similar approaches are a part of current Russian doctrine or thinking is not known, it seems likely that questions of the theory, strategy, and doctrine of nuclear weapons use will be debated in Russia for some time to come.

The debates over the role of nuclear weapons have been reflected (and to some extent reflect) bureaucratic struggles over the status of nuclear weapons forces, especially the Strategic Rocket Forces (SRF) in the Russian military. The appointment by Boris Yeltsin of Igor' Sergeev as defense minister suggested that the SRF would enjoy a period of relative prosperity and healthy funding, as Sergeev, who served for many years as the commander-in-chief of the SRF, was widely seen as favoring his former organization. Indeed, early in Sergeev's tenure the SRF enjoyed some bureaucratic gains: the space defense troops and missile early-warning system were merged with the SRF, and in late 1998, the Strategic Deterrence Force was established, which added to this structure naval strategic nuclear forces, long-range aviation, and the MoD 12th Directorate, which is responsible for nuclear weapons design, production, and control.[67]

By mid-2000, however, Sergeev was involved in an increasingly public debate with General Staff Chief Kvashnin, who favored downgrading the prestige (and funding) of the strategic nuclear forces in favor of conventional force development and reducing the size of strategic nuclear forces. In August 2000, Putin announced a plan to give

---

[65]Kipp, "Russia's Nonstrategic Nuclear Weapons."

[66]Olga Bozh'eva, "Exercises: Commonwealth-2001," *Armeiskii Sbornik,* No. 10, October 2001; Petr Polkovnikov, "CIS prepares to defeat aggression from three directions," *Nezavisimoye Voyennoye Obozreniye,* August 28, 2001.

[67]Kipp, "Russia's Nonstrategic Nuclear Weapons."

funding priority to conventional forces, per Kvashnin's wishes. At that time, there were also discussions of subordinating the SRF to the air force. While this did not happen, reshuffling in 2001 did result in a bureaucratic downgrade of the SRF and the removal of the Missile Defense and Space Defense forces from under its command.[68]

The result appears to be a comprehensive lowering of the SRF's profile. A new SRF commander named in early 2001, Nikolai Solovtzov, lacks the influence of his predecessor, Vladimir Yakovlev, and was reportedly asked by the MoD leadership to limit his public activities so as not to call attention (public or Duma) to the rocket forces' problems He appears to have done so admirably. More broadly, the MoD seems to be turning its attention to the naval nuclear forces. Reactivated construction of ballistic missiles for submarines was planned for 2002, and in January 2002, First Deputy General Staff Chief Yuriy Baluevskiy stated that Russia's new nuclear concept calls for a naval systems construction priority.[69]

There are, of course, force structure implications. With the decision, financing to support the combat readiness of the SS-19s (RS-18s) has been cut. Moreover, plans in the late 1990s to produce and deploy 10 to 20 of the new Topol-M (SS-27) missiles each year (and, in fact, ramping up to numbers as high as 40 or 50 per year[70]) appear to have been reassessed as of 2001. Only six were deployed that year—less than a full regiment. It is unclear what the system's future is, but the 2002 program does not bode well for it.[71] In the meantime, the Russian ballistic missile arsenal is aging, and the service life of many missiles is set to expire over the next few years. Service life extension, which Russian officials have suggested may be carried out for at least some of these missiles, is not particularly difficult (partly a matter of paperwork). However, the fact remains that most of Russia's ICBMs

---

[68]"'The building of the armed forces will respond to the needs of the time,' interview with Russian Defense Minister Sergei Ivanov," *Krasnaya Zvezda*, August 10 2001; Khodarenok, "Does Russia need air-space defense?"; "The Russian Army Will Become Triune," *Emerging Markets Database (Izvestia Press Digest)*, April 18, 2001.

[69]Sergei Sokut, "Russia changes its conception for building nuclear forces," *Nezavisimoye Voyennoye Obozreniye*, January 19, 2002.

[70]Pavel Podvig, "Russian Nuclear Forces in Ten Years With and Without START II," PONARS, 1999.

[71]Sokut, "Russia changes its conception for building nuclear forces."

(all except the Topol-Ms and 105 SS-19s) will become less reliable over time even if they remain deployed.[72]

Of course, as Sergei Sokut points out, this is just the latest in a series of changes in how the Russian government views and prioritizes its strategic nuclear forces. It is entirely possible that future years will bring further changes and reversals, and, as Sokut notes, this will be particularly detrimental to the quality of the force—production lines need more time to adjust than do bureaucratic (or strategic) imperatives.[73]

Russia regularly notifies the United States of the status and force structure of its strategic nuclear forces, and this information is publicly available. Conversely, little information is readily available on the number, condition, or deployment of Russian tactical (non-strategic, or, sometimes in Russian parlance, "operational" nuclear weapons). Reports of the cessation of tactical weapons production in 1992 were called into question by later statements by Russian officials. Similarly, the schedules of dismantlement and destruction of tactical weapons, as pledged in unilateral Soviet/Russian presidential nuclear initiatives in 1991 and 1992, are somewhat vague.

In 1991, Gorbachev promised to eliminate all nuclear artillery munitions, nuclear mines (the existence of which had been denied in Soviet times), and nuclear warheads for tactical missiles. He also pledged to withdraw warheads from air defense troops and remove tactical nuclear weapons from surface ships, land-based naval aviation, and multipurpose submarines. Some of these weapons were to be eliminated, the rest centrally stored. In 1992, Yeltsin reported that production of nuclear mines, artillery shells, and warheads for land-based tactical missiles had been stopped and he reaffirmed Gorbachev's pledge that these weapons would be eliminated. He also pledged to eliminate one-third of sea-based tactical nuclear systems and one-half each of the nuclear warheads designated for antiaircraft missiles and air-launched tactical nuclear munitions. [74]

---

[72]Podvig, "Russian Nuclear Forces in Ten Years With and Without START II"; Sokut, "Russia changes its conception for building nuclear forces."

[73]Sokut, "Russia changes its conception for building nuclear forces."

[74]Ivan Safranchuk, *The Future of the Russian Nuclear Arsenal*, Study Paper No. 10, PIR Center, Moscow, 1999; Yost, "Russia's Non-Strategic Nuclear Forces."

Since that time, estimates of the rate of Russian tactical nuclear weapons dismantlement, and of the remaining arsenal, have varied widely. Russian officials have claimed that nonstrategic nuclear weapons dismantlement is ongoing, at a rate of 2000 annually, but as the Congressional Research Service (CRS) points out, with no verification mechanisms, it is impossible to know if this is so. Estimates of the number of tactical warheads currently deployed also vary. The Natural Resources Defense Council (NRDC) estimated 4000 in 1998. The number stockpiled, however, may be as high as 30,000 according to some sources (the NRDC estimated 12,000).[75] All ground-based tactical weapons have reportedly been withdrawn from field units to storage, but it is not known whether they are in MoD storage sites or in those controlled by the Ministry of Atomic Energy (MinAtom).

The status of many specific systems is also unclear. In 1993 and 1994, Russian officials pledged that the nuclear mines would be gone by 1998. In 1997, it was reported that these weapons had been entirely "decommissioned," begging the question of whether or not they had been destroyed.[76] As recently as October 2001, Igor' Volynkin, of the Ministry of Defense (and chief of the directorate responsible for the nuclear arsenal), said that all of Russia's 84 nuclear munitions 30 kg or smaller were either destroyed or firmly under control.[77] Because he was responding to the famous claims of the late General Lebed' that some number of small nuclear munitions were missing, and given that Lebed' is generally believed to have had the nuclear mines in mind, this suggests that at least some of the mines have yet to be destroyed.

According to Russian nuclear specialist Ivan Safranchuk, one of the very few civilian specialists who has taken an in-depth look at Russia's tactical nuclear arsenal, the only weapons that Russia declares as fully "decommissioned" are these land mines and artillery-fired atomic projectiles. Officials have been vague about the status of

---

[75]Yost, "Russia's Non-Strategic Nuclear Forces."

[76]Ivan Safranchuk, *The Future of the Russian Nuclear Arsenal*, Study Paper No. 10, PIR Center, Moscow, 1999.

[77]"Volynkin Says Russia Knows Where Its Nuclear Weapons Are," *RFE/RL Newsline*, Vol. 5, No. 205, Part I, October 29, 2001.

naval and air weapons, suggesting the possibility that some number and combination of other land-based weapons are still deployed. These weapons include surface-to-air missiles and short-range surface-to-surface missiles; sea-based weapons such as depth-bombs, torpedoes, and cruise missiles; and air-delivered weapons such as bombs, cruise missiles, torpedoes, and depth bombs.[78] Certainly the discussions of tactical nuclear use referred to above assume ready access to a wide range of nonstrategic nuclear weaponry, including all of those mentioned here, as well as the ostensibly "decommissioned" mines.[79]

COMMAND AND CONTROL AND THE DANGER OF INADVERTENT NUCLEAR USE

As Stephen J. Cimbala writes, when it comes to deployed weapons, it is the lower echelons that have actual custody and thus at least some capacity to make decisions (this is no less the case in the United States). For the most part, this is a question of veto power, unless the weapons lack control devices or if those who have the weapons in their custody also possess the launch codes. In fact, whoever has the launch codes, whatever their position in the hierarchy, could presumably transmit an order to launch, authorized or not.[80]

According to Cimbala, Russian operational practice allows less than five minutes to detect an attack and the same amount of time to decide what to do about it.[81] Russia's early warning system has deteriorated significantly from the Soviet system, with many key components now based on the soil of other post-Soviet states.[82] Moreover, power shutdowns to key military bases—such as occurred in 1999 and 2000 in Altai, Khabarovsk, and elsewhere—can hamstring the

---

[78]Safranchuk, *The Future of the Russian Nuclear Arsenal.*

[79]See Levshin, Nedelin, and Sosnovskiy, "Use of nuclear weapons to de-escalate military operations." For an English-language synopsis, see Kipp, "Russia's Nonstrategic Nuclear Weapons."

[80]Stephen J. Cimbala, "Russia's Nuclear Command and Control: Mission Malaise," *The Journal of Slavic Military Studies,* Vol. 14, No. 2, June 2001.

[81]Ibid.

[82]Aleksandr A. Konovalov, "What should Russia's nuclear policy be?" *Emerging Markets Database (Nezavisimaya Gazeta),* April 7, 1998.

early warning systems at those locations.[83]   Obviously, problems with the early warning network and command and control system increase the danger of an accident or inadvertent launch. This is a particular concern if, as Cimbala writes, the Russian system remains geared to ensuring retaliation in the event of surprise attack (rather than to preventing accidental launch). The experience of January 1995, when the launch of a Norwegian scientific rocket alerted Russia's early warning system and resulted in a Russian strategic alert, provides a caution. Although weapons were not launched, it was reported that system malfunction caused parts of Russia's arsenal to go into combat mode independently.[84]

If all is working properly, the launch of strategic nuclear weapons by Russia would require a top-level presidential decision. In theory, so would the use of tactical nuclear weapons. However, it appears that once deployed, many tactical nuclear weapons are functionally beyond central control (with the exception of air-delivered weapons, which are generally stored away from the delivery system). That is, operators may have more than just veto authority over weapons launch but *de facto* discretion over their use. Because the authority under which ground-based tactical systems are stored is unclear (i.e., whether these weapons are in MoD or MinAtom storage sites), *de facto* release authority is another mystery. Even *de jure* control is not entirely clear. Safranchuk believes that some changes to the command and control system might have been made in the late 1990s, when Russia reorganized into seven military districts. On paper, the military district commanders have full authority over all military forces deployed on their territory. Safranchuk doubts that this includes nuclear weapons, but because these were not mentioned in the reorganization, he postulates that perhaps classified directives address the relationship between the center and military districts regarding the nuclear arsenal.[85]

Because both MoD and MinAtom weapon-storage facilities are widely believed to be secure and reliable, and because of the physical difficulties of removing and using a weapon from these facilities,

---

[83]Sokov, "The Reality and Myths of Nuclear Regionalism in Russia."

[84]Cimbala, "Russia's Nuclear Command and Control."

[85]Author discussion with Ivan Safranchuk, June 19, 2000.

there is little real risk of theft or diversion of nuclear weapons from Russian storage sites.[86] The more significant threat is potential intentional use by military units, with or without authorization from the central authorities in Moscow. In the event of an armed conflict, a commander who has such weapons at his disposal could be tempted to use them were the situation to turn dire. In fact, the de-escalation doctrine proposed in the pages of military journals and discussed in the preceding section posits almost this very turn of events. While the initial use of a nuclear weapon requires a decision by the commander in chief (president) and a direct order from the Minister of Defense or General Staff chief, secondary and tertiary strike authority is delegated lower and lower down the chain of command.[87]

Moreover, although the strategic weapons are assigned to and commanded by the central SRF, many of the tactical weapons, once deployed, may well be in the field commander's hands. Little is known about Russian tactical nuclear command and control, safety, and security, but there is reason to question whether any physical means exist that would prevent such a field commander from using certain deployed naval or ground forces weapons. The fundamental question is whether unlocking codes exist, and, if so, at what level of authority they can be accessed. If there are weapons for which there are no such codes or if the tactical commander can access them, even if that commander is in principle obligated to wait for a presidential decision prior to any nuclear use, in practice there could well be the risk that someone, sometime, may be able to decide independently to employ a nuclear weapon without such authorization.

---

[86]Safranchuk, "Be prepared for nuclear terror" (in Russian), *Itogi*, October 12, 1999; author conversation with Ivan Safranchuk, June 19, 2000; and author conversation with Paul Podvig, June 19, 2000. The Russian Ministry of Defense now uses officers rather than enlisted men to guard nuclear weapons transport, perhaps because of incidents (as noted in recent press reports) in which two students were dismissed for drug use from a training center for nuclear weapons facility guards and another in which sentries on guard duty while transporting nuclear weapons left their posts. (Maxim Kniazkov, "U.S. Certifies Theft of Russian Nuclear Material Has Occurred," *Johnson's Russia List* [AFP], February 25, 2002.)

[87]Levshin, Nedelin, and Sosnovskiy, "Use of nuclear weapons to de-escalate military operations."

Chapter Seven

WEAK LINKS: ROAD, RAIL, AND NUCLEAR POWER

TRANSPORT AND DISTRIBUTION

Russia's transportation network is a critical variable in both the likelihood of crisis and the ease of its resolution. Throughout the 1990s, there were worries about the state of the road and rail network that connects Russia's vast territory. For example, a 1998 study by the Russian Academy of Sciences found that investment in basic infrastructure in the 1990s was barely 25 percent of the 1989 Soviet level.[1] The most immediate and visible problems for Russia's road networks are geographically centered in the Far East. Not a single surfaced road runs all the way across the country. An attempt to drive to the Pacific coast east of Lake Baykal would encounter numerous gaps requiring long detours and/or specialized vehicles. The remainder of Russia, where the federal highway system is much more developed, poses a different problem. Highways throughout the country are operating at two to three times their designed capacity in terms of volume and load weight; if overused roads continue to go without maintenance or upgrades, commercial road travel and transport between Russia's more populated west and south may become difficult or even impossible within the next ten years.

Concerns have also been raised about the state of Russia's railways. In the mid-1990s, the Cooperative Threat Reduction (CTR) program of the U.S. government, which assisted Russia with nuclear disman-

---

[1]Fred Weir, "Triple Disaster to Destroy Russia in 2003 Says Duma Commission," *The Independent,* September 24, 2000, p. A1.

tlements in accordance with existing agreements, offered to provide additional fire-suppression equipment for rail cars used to transport nuclear weapons. At that time, Russian authorities voiced fears that rail cars would then be excessively heavy, and asked whether the United States would provide equipment to enable them to detect defective track.[2] Whether or not that request was rooted in real needs, defective track has been a concern throughout Russia's rail network because there has been little investment in maintenance of Russia's railroad beds. However, a revival of traffic in the past year or so and better financial returns have facilitated a doubling of investment, which this year is expected to grow another 50 percent. It is claimed that increased spending on maintenance has already put the track in much better shape.[3]

It is plausible, however, that continued deterioration will cause Russia's road and rail system to experience temporary breakdowns which, in a worst-case scenario, could temporarily isolate towns or even entire regions from commercial traffic. If combined with disease or conflict, isolation could conceivably contribute to a humanitarian disaster. However, Russia's networks should certainly be adequate for a capable military to mobilize to stem a conflict or crisis, either within or on the borders of the Russian federation. The largest problem that ground transportation in Russia faces is simply distance and the inherent challenges of mobilizing across long distances in time to meet an urgent need.

POWER PLANTS AND OTHER CIVILIAN AND MILITARY NUCLEAR FACILITIES

As already discussed, Russia's nuclear weapons for the most part appear to be under secure control. However, Russia is also home to a vast network of reactors, research laboratories, and other facilities

---

[2]U.S. General Accounting Office, *Weapons of Mass Destruction: Reducing the Threat from the Former Soviet Union*, Letter Report, GAO/NSIAD-95-7, October 6, 1994.

[3]Author conversation with Robert North, specialist in the Russian rail network, and *Zeleznodorozhny Transport* 2000, No. 1, pp. 9, 11, 13.

that produce, use, and store nuclear materials for both military and civilian purposes.[4]

There are two families of fears that arise from Russia's civilian nuclear complexes. One is the risk of material "leakage"—the danger that unauthorized persons could acquire some amount of nuclear material, which they could then use to manufacture a weapon. This threat is not relevant to most of Russia's civilian reactors (with one notable exception[5]), which neither use nor produce material in a form readily usable in a weapon. However, it is cause for concern at a wide range of research and weapons-related facilities. Moreover, there remains the threat of someone acquiring radioactive material that is not suitable for fabricating a weapon but that could be used by terrorists to contaminate an airfield, a business district, or a local water supply.

No component of Russia's nuclear industry is immune to the second family of threats—that associated with accidents or sabotage. There are a number of ways in which accidental or purposeful release of radioactive material from one or another nuclear-related facility could place public health and welfare at risk. Past accidents at Russian nuclear facilities in the Urals have led to high levels of environmental contamination and illness. While the 1986 Chornobyl disaster in Ukraine is the best known of the Soviet accidents, cases of radioactive leakage and poor safety procedures have led to contamination in areas throughout the former USSR.[6] As the infrastructure ages and the facilities continue to operate, the dangers increase.

No one can argue that this potential for problems in Russia's nuclear sector, civilian and military, has been ignored. The U.S. Department of Defense's CTR program has been a tremendously successful

---

[4]Facilities deemed a potential proliferation risk, with key information about each one, are listed in Jon Brook Wolfsthal, Cristina-Astrid Chuen, and Emily Ewell Daughtry (eds.), *Nuclear Status Report: Nuclear Weapons, Fissile Material, and Export Controls in the Former Soviet Union*, Monterey Institute of International Studies and Carnegie Endowment for International Peace, Monterey, California, and Washington, DC, 2001, pp. 75–157.

[5]The BN-600 reactor, discussed below.

[6]See D. J. Bradley, *Behind the Nuclear Curtain: Radioactive Waste Management in the Former Soviet Union*, Battelle Press, Columbus, Ohio, 1997.

means of providing assistance to Russia to ensure that weapons dismantlement proceeds in line with arms control commitments. Other U.S. initiatives to support nonproliferation and arms control goals have involved the purchase of highly enriched uranium (HEU), plans to burn weapons plutonium as fuel in civilian power reactors, and the planned conversion of plutonium production reactors to civilian use. The U.S. Departments of Energy and Defense have worked with Russia's military and civilian (and dual) research laboratories and nuclear weapons–related facilities to improve security. To help lower the risk of accident, the Department of Energy (DoE) and Nuclear Regulatory Commission (NRC) have worked hand in hand with their counterparts in the federation to improve safety controls at civilian nuclear reactors and to urge the federation to shut down the oldest, least-safe systems.[7]

But the task at hand is gargantuan, and even as efforts continue, so does deterioration. The nuclear power reactors, for example, suffer not only from age but from a Soviet legacy that gave little regard to individual human life and health. The facilities were built to maximize energy produced, not safety. While the Chornobyl explosion in 1986 is the only well-known case of an accident at a Soviet-made reactor, small and large-scale catastrophes have plagued the Soviet (now Russian and other successor states') nuclear power sector since the 1950s. Most of these accidents have been related to waste and reprocessing facilities, but power reactors are in no way immune, as recent examples show. In September 2000, for instance, an unexpected blackout caused by a fault in the electrical grid triggered the shutdown of three nuclear reactors in the Urals—the BN-600 at the Beloyarsk nuclear power plant and two at the Mayak reprocessing facility. The reactors appear to have shut down automatically, but there was a half-hour delay before backup electricity supply systems designed to cool the reactors in an emergency began functioning at Mayak. Mayak chief Vitaliy Sadovnikov described the blackout as the worst in his plant's experience and praised his staff for averting a catastrophe that some specialists say would have been "another Chornobyl." Less sensational but still worrisome were reports in 2000 by Russia's nuclear-monitoring agency, GosAtomNadzor

---

[7]An overview of U.S. nonproliferation assistance is provided in Wolfsthal, Chuen, and Daughtry (eds.), *Nuclear Status Report*, pp. 47–74.

(GAN), that flaws in the metal in the pipes in several reactors could lead to radioactive material leakage.[8]

Of the 29 nuclear power reactor units (at nine separate locations) operational in Russia today, 19 represent models that international experts have deemed irredeemably unsafe. These include the "Chornobyl-type" RBMK (light water-cooled, graphite-moderated) reactors, a similar system in the Far East's nuclear power plant, and early model VVER pressurized-water reactors. Not included in the 29 but providing power to the surrounding region are two military plutonium production reactors, one at Tomsk and one at Krasnoyarsk. These systems are similar to the RBMK, but because they produce plutonium, they pose proliferation risks as well as safety concerns. The BN-600 fast breeder reactor at Beloyarsk, although a civilian reactor and generally a safe model, also produces plutonium that could be used in a nuclear weapon.[9]

Although the specific fault that enabled the Chornobyl accident has been remedied at all such reactors, other factors that make the older Russian reactors unsafe are far more difficult to fix. These factors vary by system but include the absence of containment structures such as the one that prevented massive radiation leakage after the 1979 accident at Three Mile Island in the United States. Another problem is that the RBMK is designed so that if cooling water is lost, the nuclear chain reaction speeds up, rather than slowing down and stopping as in newer, safer systems. The older-model VVERs, for their part, lack emergency core-cooling or auxiliary feedwater systems, and are susceptible to gradual weakening of the reactor pressure vessel that surrounds the nuclear fuel. Finally, the Russian reactors were generally built to far lower construction and safety standards than is the Western norm.[10]

---

[8]Jan Cleave, "Violations of Nuclear Safety Regulations Totaled 840 Last Year," *RFE/RL Newsline*, Vol. 4, No. 91, Part I, May 11, 2000; Igor Kudrik, "Three Reactors Black Out," *Bellona: Accidents and Incidents*, September 12, 2000, http://www.bellona.no/ imaker?id=17859&sub=1; Amelia Gentleman, Nuclear Disaster Averted," *The Observer* (UK), September 17, 2000.

[9]Author discussions with Russian officials; U.S. General Accounting Office, *Nuclear Safety: Concerns with the Continuing Operation of Soviet-Designed Nuclear Power Reactors*, GAO/RCED-00-97; Tony Weslowsky, "Risky Business," *Bulletin of the Atomic Scientists*, Vol. 57, No. 3, May/June 2001.

[10]Weslowsky, *Soviet-Designed Nuclear Power Reactors*.

Despite Western efforts to convince Russia to shut down these old and dangerous reactors, all of them continue in operation. Not a single reactor has been decommissioned since 1990. Indeed, Russian officials have sought to justify their refusal to end production at these facilities by pointing to the safety assistance that Western donors have provided, which they argue has made the reactors safe to operate.[11] In 2000, RosEnergoAtom director Boris Antonov assured the Russian public that all of Russia's reactors were safe and must meet some of the world's most stringent standards and regulations to operate.[12] However, four of Russia's 29 nuclear reactors continue to operate today despite having reached their 30-year service limit in 2001. Ten more will reach that point by 2007. While service life can be extended with upgrades and modernization, some measure of which has taken place (and is taking place), with current fund shortages and cost uncertainties, it is not known whether these fixes will be sufficient to guarantee the "100 percent" level of safety that Antonov claims exists.[13]

Russian unwillingness to end the operation of what are most likely unsafe reactors is rooted in Russia's need for the energy they provide. Although Russia as a whole gets only about 14 percent of its total energy from nuclear power, this figure is misleading. While in the Far East a single nuclear power plant provides very little of the region's energy, the fraction grows as one moves west: central Russia relies on nuclear production for one-third of its energy and northwest Russia depends on its three nuclear power plants for half of its electricity.[14]

---

[11]U.S. General Accounting Office, *Nuclear Safety: Concerns with the Continuing Operation of Soviet-Designed Nuclear Power Reactors*, GAO/RCED-00-97.

[12]Nikolai Ivanov, "'Russian Nuclear Power Stations Meet Most Stringent International Standards,'" *Nezavisimaya Gazeta*, April 11, 2000.

[13]"Four Nuclear Reactors to Reach Service Limit in 2001," *Interfax Daily Business Report*, December 24, 1999; Ivanov, "'Russian Nuclear Power Stations Meet Most Stringent International Standards.'"

[14]Tony Weslowsky, "Russia: Nuclear Power Plans Move Forward," http://search.rferl.org/nca/features/1999/02/F.RU.990222144021.html; *Source Book: Soviet-Designed Nuclear Power Plants in Russia, Ukraine, Lithuania, Armenia, the Czech Republic, the Slovak Republic, Hungary and Bulgaria*, Nuclear Energy Institute, Washington, DC, 1997, p. 105; *Country Analysis Brief: Russia* [Internet edition], Energy Information Agency, U.S. Department of Energy, October 2001 (cited February 23, 2002), available from http://www.eia.doe.gov/emeu/cabs/russia.html.

This reliance on nuclear energy combines with financial constraints to keep the old reactors running. Although Russian officials have said that they plan to complete five reactors begun under Soviet rule and build 25 new ones over the next two decades, it is questionable whether the funds to do so exist.[15] Although Russia sells reactor technology and equipment abroad, such sales have not been sufficient to support the level of financing necessary to build new electric power reactors at home. Thus, even reactors as old and dangerous as the two VVER-440/230s at the Novovoronezh site, whose warranted lifespans are expired or expiring, will very likely be kept in operation as its operators seek approval to put off the mandatory shutdown date by a few more years.[16]

An even more dangerous situation is posed by the three plutonium production reactors that continue to operate in Russia. Part of both the civilian energy infrastructure and the weapons-grade plutonium cycle, these reactors produce weapons plutonium as well as energy to the surrounding region. The reactors are similar in design to the Chornobyl-type RBMK reactor, although they are a great deal older. The combination of security concerns, arms control, and proliferation concerns related to continued plutonium production led the United States and Russia to sign a series of agreements regarding these reactors dating from 1994. Initially, the reactors were to be shut down by 2000, but a revised 1997 agreement allowed them to continue in operation until conversion in 2002/2003 would cease their production of plutonium. Various conversion plans failed to win approval, however, and the reactors continue in operation largely unmodified and increasingly unsafe. The most recent statements by Russia, in August 2001, admitted that the country lacked the resources to phase out reactors by 2002/2003 as planned and that the reactors would instead continue in operation through 2005 and 2006.[17]

---

[15]*Country Analysis Brief.*

[16]Author discussions with Russian officials; U.S. General Accounting Office, *Nuclear Safety: Concerns with the Continuing Operation of Soviet-Designed Nuclear Power Reactors*, GAO/RCED-00-97.

[17]Rashid Alimov, *Russia Reviews Terms of Pu Reprocessing Reduction*, Bellona.no, August 31, 2001 (cited February 26, 2002); "Moscow Wants More Time to Phase Out Plutonium Reactors," *RFE/RL Newsline*, Vol. 5, No. 163, Part I, August 28, 2001; Sokov, "The Reality and Myths of Nuclear Regionalism in Russia."

The regional dimension plays a role here, too. Nikolai Sokov argues that an alliance has emerged between MinAtom and governors who have MinAtom facilities in their regions. Those governors support the expansion of nuclear power and the development of fuel reprocessing, which bolsters MinAtom's ability to advance its interests vis-à-vis the federal government. Both MinAtom and the governors see this as a way to counter the federally controlled Unified Energy System (RAO EES), which has a monopoly over power distribution and generation (and which MinAtom believes underprices nuclear energy). So far, joint efforts have involved cooperation between MinAtom and Cheliabinks Oblast leaders to complete the South Urals nuclear power plant opposed by local ecological activists and a 1999 intervention by the governor of Tomsk Oblast after GAN closed down one of the plutonium-producing reactors. The reactor was restarted, and Sokov writes that it is not known whether it was repaired to meet the GAN criteria that led it to be closed in the first place.[18] Most recently, MinAtom subsidiary RosEnergoAtom has announced that it is creating a new electric power company, Unified Generating Company (EKG), to compete with EES. It will be responsible for consolidating the power output of ten nuclear power stations.[19]

In sum, it seems unlikely that Russia will cease to rely on nuclear power in the foreseeable future. In fact, lacking the funding for new full-scale power plants, Russian officials have discussed plans to solve at least some of the Far East's energy shortage problems by placing a number of "floating" nuclear reactors off the region's coastlines. Construction could begin as early as 2002, although at the time of this writing it is unclear whether GAN had fully approved the design, which is based on the reactors that power Russia's icebreaker ships and is similar in principle to a small VVER (and reasonably safe).[20]

---

[18]Sokov, "The Reality and Myths of Nuclear Regionalism in Russia."

[19]"Atomic Energy Ministry Creates Own Power Company," *RFE/RL Newsline*, Vol. 6, No. 34, Part I, February 21, 2002.

[20]Author discussions with Russian officials and specialists; "Russia possesses 35 designs for low-capacity nuclear reactors," World Nuclear Association News Briefing, October 10, 2001 (cited February 23, 2002); available from http://www.world-nuclear.org/nb/nb01/nb0142.htm.

Concerns about aging equipment are not unique to the civilian power reactor sector. Other nuclear facilities face similar problems as well as additional proliferation risks. The facilities in question include the three plutonium production reactors mentioned above; plutonium reprocessing sites; nuclear weapons design and assembly facilities; and research, training, and experimental nuclear reactors. Also of concern is Russia's fleet of nuclear-powered ships (predominantly submarines and icebreakers), whose waste and damaged reactors have often been dumped at sea. Risk of accident or material diversion at such facilities, as with the nuclear power plants, is exacerbated by the poor pay, housing, and conditions faced by workers in the nuclear sector. Other Russian industrial workers face similar conditions, but poor performance and dissatisfaction here may have far more severe repercussions.

Security at Russian nuclear-related facilities varies widely. Some, such as research laboratories that have received considerable Western assistance, have modern key-code systems in place. All of Russia's nuclear facilities, including reactors (which, with the exception of the Balakovo reactor, have received Western assistance geared more to safety than security), have multiple checkpoints for identity confirmation as personnel enter the facility. Security at nuclear power plants has also been upgraded in the face of threats by Chechen rebels in the late 1990s to sabotage the plants.

But Western efforts have also met with roadblocks. Some are rooted in the long history of secrecy surrounding the Russian nuclear complex. For instance, DoE has identified 252 buildings at 40 locations in Russia that require security systems to protect nuclear materials. These include civilian sites, components of the nuclear weapons complex, and naval facilities. As of February 2001, DoE had been able to partially or completely install security upgrades and systems at 115 buildings. These buildings contain just under one-third of the weapons-usable nuclear material that DoE has deemed as at risk of theft or diversion. DoE reports that it is expanding these measures to other facilities. Unfortunately, another 104 civilian and military buildings that have been identified as housing hundreds of metric tons of this material remain closed to DoE by the Ministry of Atomic Energy. Because most of them are components of the Russian nuclear weapons laboratory complex, prospects for access do not look good.[21]

Another problem that prevents progress at both civilian and military facilities is more psychological than bureaucratic in nature. It is one aspect of the absence of a safety "culture" that Westerners often cite as a problem among Russian specialists. Many note that while Russian officials are willing to improve controls to guard against outsiders, there is an unwillingness to accept the possibility of an "insider" threat. Russians place a great deal of faith in the integrity, honesty, and patriotism of the professionals that work in this area. Officials stress the high levels of education of nuclear facility workers, and few are willing to give much credence to the risk of someone on the inside contributing to the diversion of materials.[22]

Many Russians will also dismiss the extent of the threat of diversion by pointing out the difficulties of diverting high-grade nuclear material from a nuclear power plant or research facility. They emphasize that only the BN-600, the plutonium production reactors, and some research reactors pose proliferation threats. Furthermore, they argue that at both civilian and other facilities, there are safety and security systems in place, and even those that received no Western attention have functioned adequately for years. Outsiders would require some logistical preparation to obtain entry into the facility and knowledge about the material in question—its handling and characteristics.

These arguments have some validity but are also somewhat misleading. Reports of the difficulty of accessing Russian facilities are contradicted by the fact that officials have intercepted small amounts of high-grade nuclear material traceable to Russian nuclear (generally research) facilities. In almost all of these cases, some insider in-

---

[21]U.S. General Accounting Office, *Nuclear Nonproliferation: Security of Russia's Nuclear Material Improving; Further Enhancements Needed*, GAO-01-312. The GAO also reports some problems with the implementation of the security procedures, although overall DoE is improving the security of material in Russia.

[22]Author discussions with Russian officials and specialists. This problem is also noted by William C. Potter and Fred L. Wehling in "Sustainability: A Vital Component of Nuclear Material Security in Russia," *The Nonproliferation Review*, Vol. 7, No. 1, Spring 2000.

volvement was confirmed.[23] The problem of theft and diversion is exacerbated by Russia's poor system of accounting for its nuclear materials. It is reasonably likely that no one would notice a successful theft until long after the event. Furthermore, arguments about the difficulty of handling and using nuclear material are overstated. The way plutonium and highly enriched uranium are usually stored makes them reasonably easy and safe to handle. If one possesses the knowledge, expertise, and facilities, one could create a nuclear explosion with as little as 2.2 lb of plutonium or 5.5 of HEU (less knowledge requires larger amounts, but a crude weapon can be fashioned with a little over 100 lb of HEU).[24]

It is true that most nuclear power plants, as already noted, do not pose much of a proliferation risk. Steps taken in recent years make accident or sabotage less likely as well. Low levels of computerization at the plants, for example, provide security against hackers who might seek to disrupt the system.[25] But lower risk is not no risk, and it does not require a bomb to wage nuclear terror. As Ivan Safranchuk suggests in an October 1999 article, it may be possible for a terrorist to acquire a small quantity of radioactive materials, perhaps purchasing them from a disgruntled plant or research laboratory worker, and use them to pollute or threaten to pollute the water or air in a given location.[26] A November 2001 statement issued by MinAtom may be a promising sign of increased recognition of the threat. The statement said that MinAtom wants to expand cooperation with U.S. nuclear labs with a specific focus on improving security arrangements at Russian facilities. The program proposed includes regular safety exercises, better communications, and

---

[23]Center for Nonproliferation Studies at the Monterey Institute of International Studies and the Non-Proliferation Project at the Carnegie Endowment for International Peace, *Nuclear Successor States of the Soviet Union: Status Report on Nuclear Weapons, Fissile Material and Export Controls*, No. 5, March 1998, http://cns.miis.edu/pubs/reports/statrep.htm, pp. 105–110.

[24]Graham T. Allison, Owen R. Coté, Jr., Richard A. Falkenrath, and Steven E. Miller, *Avoiding Nuclear Anarchy: Containing the Threat of Loose Russian Nuclear Weapons and Fissile Material*, The MIT Press, Cambridge, Massachusetts, 1996, pp. 44–45.

[25]Author discussion with Mikhail Ivanovich Miroshnichenko, deputy chief of the Nuclear and Radiation Safety Department, GosAtomNadzor, June 15, 2000.

[26]Safranchuk, "Be prepared for nuclear terror."

monitoring of critical sites.[27] In the meantime, testimony by CIA director George Tenet to the U.S. Congress revealed that the U.S. intelligence community believes that weapons-grade and weapons-usable nuclear material has been stolen from Russian nuclear-related facilities in recent years. Specific cases of theft of materials that remain unaccounted for are noted, and there may well be others.[28]

---

[27]"Atomic Energy Minister Wants to Expand Security Cooperation with U.S.," *RFE/RL Newsline*, Vol. 5, No. 217, Part I, November 15, 2001.

[28]Kniazkov, "U.S. Certifies Theft of Russian Nuclear Material Has Occurred."

Chapter Eight

ILLUSTRATIVE SCENARIOS

The preceding chapters have illustrated the ways in which Russia's decline affects that country and may evolve into challenges and dangers that extend well beyond its borders. The political factors of decline may make Russia a less stable international actor and other factors may increase the risk of internal unrest. Together and separately, they increase the risk of conflict and the potential scope of other imaginable disasters. The trends of regionalization, particularly the disparate rates of economic growth among regions combined with the politicization of regional economic and military interests, will be important to watch. The potential for locale, or possibly ethnicity, to serve as a rallying point for internal conflict is low at present, but these factors have the potential to feed into precisely the cycle of instability that political scientists have identified as making states in transition to democracy more likely to become involved in war. These factors also increase the potential for domestic turmoil, which further increases the risk of international conflict, for instance if Moscow seeks to unite a divided nation and/or demonstrate globally that its waning power remains something to be reckoned with.

Given Russia's conventional weakness, an increased risk of conflict carries with it an increased risk of nuclear weapons use, and Russia's demographic situation increases the potential for a major epidemic with possible implications for Europe and perhaps beyond. The dangers posed by Russia's civilian and military nuclear weapons complex, aside from the threat of nuclear weapons use, create a real risk of proliferation of weapons or weapons materials to terrorist groups, as well as perpetuating an increasing risk of accident at one of Russia's nuclear power plants or other facilities.

These elements touch upon key security interests, thus raising serious concerns for the United States. A declining Russia increases the likelihood of conflict—internal or otherwise—and the general deterioration that Russia has in common with "failing" states raises serious questions about its capacity to respond to an emerging crisis. A crisis in large, populous, and nuclear-armed Russia can easily affect the interests of the United States and its allies. In response to such a scenario, the United States, whether alone or as part of a larger coalition, could be asked to send military forces to the area in and around Russia. This chapter will explore a handful of scenarios that could call for U.S. involvement.

A wide range of crisis scenarios can be reasonably extrapolated from the trends implicit in Russia's decline. A notional list includes:

- Authorized or unauthorized belligerent actions by Russian troops in trouble-prone Russian regions or in neighboring states could lead to armed conflict.

- Border clashes with China in the Russian Far East or between Russia and Ukraine, the Baltic states, Kazakhstan, or another neighbor could escalate into interstate combat.

- Nuclear-armed terrorists based in Russia or using weapons or materials diverted from Russian facilities could threaten Russia, Europe, Asia, or the United States.

- Civil war in Russia could involve fighting near storage sites for nuclear, chemical, or biological weapons and agents, risking large-scale contamination and humanitarian disaster.

- A nuclear accident at a power plant or facility could endanger life and health in Russia and neighboring states.

- A chemical accident at a plant or nuclear-related facility could endanger life and health in Russia and neighboring states.

- Ethnic pogroms in south Russia could force refugees into Georgia, Azerbaijan, Armenia, and/or Ukraine.

- Economic and ethnic conflicts in Caucasus could erupt into armed clashes, which would endanger oil and gas pipelines in the region.

- A massive ecological disaster such as an earthquake, famine, or epidemic could spawn refugees and spread illness and death across borders.

- An increasingly criminalized Russian economy could create a safe haven for crime or even terrorist-linked groups. From this base, criminals, drug traders, and terrorists could threaten the people and economies of Europe, Asia, and the United States.

- Accelerated Russian weapons and technology sales or unauthorized diversion could foster the proliferation of weapons and weapon materials to rogue states and nonstate terrorist actors, increasing the risk of nuclear war.

This list is far from exhaustive. However significant these scenarios may be, not all are relevant to U.S. military planning. We therefore applied several criteria to the larger portfolio of potential scenarios, with an eye to identifying the most useful for a more detailed discussion. First, only those scenarios that involve a reasonable threat to U.S. strategic interests were considered. Second, while it is important to plan for the unexpected, it is equally crucial to understand the likelihood of various events. We thus included a range of probabilities but eliminated those that we considered least plausible. Third, we only chose scenarios for which the Western response would likely be military or would rely on considerable military involvement. Lastly, we wanted to select a variety of situations, ones that created differing imperatives for the U.S. government and its Air Force, rather than scenarios which, while equal in significance, present fairly similar problems. We therefore offer the following four storylines as illustrative, if far from exhaustive, of the types of challenges that would be presented by operations on or near Russian territory.

WAR IN ASIA

Both conventional wisdom and the political science literature posit that substantial state decline, or the appearance thereof, can invite foreign adventurism. To date, Russia's military weakness has not been seen as an invitation for ambitious rival states to wrest away a chunk of Russian territory. Russia's large arsenal of strategic and nonstrategic nuclear weapons is no doubt a factor. This may change over the next decade or so, particularly if Russia continues to weaken and demographic trends stay on their present downward paths.

The Scenario

This scenario takes place around the year 2015 and assumes that Russia has continued to deteriorate militarily throughout the intervening period. This decline has been especially severely felt in the Far East, where troops are unfed, unpaid, and untrained, and equipment is obsolete. Chinese migration into the Far East and Russian emigration from it have continued, and significant numbers of Chinese have settled permanently in the area.

Beijing, whose military might has increased as Russia's has declined, has begun to make noises about its historic right to southeastern Russia, territory that was annexed between 1858 and 1860 from a China weakened by the Opium Wars. In 2015, with a rapidly growing Chinese population in that area (where families are unhindered by population control regulations), Beijing is able to create considerable domestic support for "reclaiming" the territory.

Domestic pressure in China to take back the "lost territories" is bolstered by an increasingly hostile Russian policy and attitude toward Chinese immigrants. Driven by ethnic tensions that have increased along with the Chinese population, laws now limit the duration and location of Chinese residency. Discrimination in employment and housing against people of East Asian ancestry is rampant. Despite this, economic opportunities attract more and more Chinese to the area. Whatever "strategic partnership" might once have been evolving between Beijing and Moscow has long disappeared and relations between the two countries are poisoned by Russian anti-Chinese sentiment and Beijing's insistence on pursuing the rights of co-ethnics living in Russia and rumblings about regaining long-lost land.

In addition to historical claims and the desire to protect the rights of ethnic Chinese, China has a strategic interest in the land southeast of the Amur River. This territory provides an outlet to the Sea of Japan, an outlet China now lacks.

China's strategy for acquiring the territory is based on a plan to pro-
voke Russia into attacking Chinese forces in the region. China,
pleading self-defense, could then counterattack into Russia. Beijing,
possessing by now a large strategic nuclear force, is confident that
Moscow will not risk nuclear war and the destruction of European
Russia to defend the poor and underpopulated Far East. The
People's Liberation Army (PLA) therefore begins to shift more forces
toward the border with Russia. The plan goes awry, however, when
Chinese forces get into a firefight with Russian border guards near
the border at the Ussuri River. Chinese commanders on the scene
seize territory in Primorsky Krai; the weak and disorganized Russian
forces in the region are able to put up little resistance. With this *fait
accompli*, Beijing orders its navy to gear up for an amphibious
landing at Vladivostok and elsewhere on the coast. See Figure 8.1.

RANDMR1442-8.1

Figure 8.1—Chinese Force Movements

Japan is alarmed by this turn of events. It sees the land grab in Russia as an example of aggressive Chinese military adventurism and feels particularly threatened by the prospect of a Chinese outlet to the Sea of Japan. After consultations, Japan and Russia decide that, given both states' relative military weakness, it is time to call on the United States for help.

Washington initially offers to mediate, but while China responds that it is willing to enter into talks, the PLA continues to shift more forces to the Russian border and ships are heading for Vladivostok. Russia therefore invokes its status as a Partnership for Peace state to request NATO consultations. Japan, in turn, asks the United States to assist in rolling back the Chinese land grab in Russia.

Implications

This scenario may at first read more like fiction than a plausible future. Projecting 15 years forward is difficult under the best of circumstances, and doing it with regard to two states in as much flux as Russia and China is particularly challenging. Furthermore, even if events were to evolve as outlined, the United States would retain freedom of choice: it would be under no obligation to intervene to defend Russia against the Chinese. On the other hand, especially if U.S.-Chinese relations continue to deteriorate, the United States may find it difficult to refuse the request of its close ally, Tokyo, and a Russia in need.

Furthermore, a conflict between Russia and China would be a clash between two nuclear weapon states. Although China has a "no first use" policy, Russia does not. This scenario posits that Beijing is betting that the nuclear taboo will hold, but one can easily imagine that a Russia that is weakened conventionally and facing a foreign incursion onto its soil may feel that it has no choice but to escalate to nuclear use.

Thus, this scenario is not likely but is included because it has serious implications for U.S. interests. While the probability of such a course of events is low, it is far from negligible, for China does have interests in the Russian Far East, and Japan (like other states in the region) is highly attuned to the possibility of Chinese adventurism.

NUCLEAR ACCIDENT

The possibility of a major mishap (whether arising from accident or deliberate sabotage) occurring at one of the many civilian and military nuclear and nuclear-related facilities in Russia is very real. The risk ranges from a Chornobyl-type power reactor accident to terrorist use of nuclear waste to contaminate a large area of Russia (or, potentially, elsewhere).

Such a catastrophe could happen almost anywhere in Russia. In European Russia it would have serious implications for many U.S. friends and allies. On the other hand, there would be numerous Western countries nearby, ready and willing to help, and fairly well-developed infrastructure to support their doing so. Further into Russia, depending on wind direction, the dangers may be limited to Russia itself or they may reach other states in Asia. In that case, deteriorated road and rail networks as well as simple distance could make the provision of aid and evacuation of the local population a very challenging task.

Regardless, it is plausible that Moscow would have difficulty coordinating a response on its own. Moreover, it would clearly be in the interest of the world community to assist in mitigating the damage, if only to ensure that it does not spread.

The Scenario

Tomorrow, or the next day, or next year, the world awakes to reports of a large-scale nuclear accident at a power plant in central or eastern Russia. It appears likely that windborne radioactive dust will reach areas in Asia outside of Russia. After initially denying that an accident has occurred, Russia admits to a minor leak of radioactive material. In the meantime, it is clear that Russian firefighters are at the site and military aircraft are evacuating people from the area. After an aircraft carrying refugees crashes in the Urals, Russia asks the world for assistance in mitigating the effects of the disaster.

Implications

The U.S. Federal Emergency Management Administration (FEMA) has had extensive discussions with its counterpart in Russia, the

Ministry of the Russian Federation for Civil Defense, Emergencies, and Elimination of Consequences of Natural Disasters (EMERCOM), precisely about such disasters and how best to respond to them. The two have conducted joint exercises and carried out planning for co-operative activity. This bodes well for their ability to work together in an actual crisis.

At the same time, in domestic emergencies FEMA relies on U.S. military—and particularly U.S. Air Force and Air National Guard—assets to carry out tasks. These same assets would be the most likely sources of support for a crisis abroad, especially if it involved a nuclear accident deep inside Russia. There would simply be no other way to traverse the huge distances quickly and effectively while evacuating people and airlifting in supplies and equipment. The large, heavy aircraft would strain existing runways and information about the condition of facilities would be imperative. Getting fuel to the area for the aircraft would be an additional challenge.

As long as Russia had issued a request for help, however, many of these problems could be mitigated: first by Moscow's cooperation and second by the ability to base out of nearby countries, where facilities might be in better condition and/or better known. On the other hand, if regional separatism has continued to evolve, operations outside the danger zone might be hampered by uncooperative local officials who equate U.S. help with Moscow's interference.[1] The prevalence of crime and corruption raise the risk of theft of fuel, supplies, or parts, as it has for Russian forces throughout the country. Furthermore, if the accident turns out to be the result of sabotage, outside intervention might be targeted by the groups responsible.

This scenario is both plausible and a near-term danger. While core U.S. interests may not be affected by an accident, the United States has a history of assisting with humanitarian missions, and it is unlikely that it would refuse to assist with one of this sort.

---

[1]An alternative scenario might involve regional officials requesting U.S. aid and Moscow proving less than cooperative.

TERRORIST USE OF NUCLEAR MATERIALS

This scenario is a common one, popular in film and fiction even before the terrorist attacks on the United States on September 11, 2001. It is also a very real danger. While most experts agree that Russian nuclear weapons, strategic and tactical, are generally under sound and reliable control, the theft or diversion of a tactical nuclear weapon is possible. Insofar as it is not known where these weapons are stored or how many of them there are, it is even possible (if not very likely) that such a diversion has already occurred. Moreover, terrorists would not need a ready-made nuclear weapon to create a real threat: if they are able to gain sufficient high-quality nuclear material and have the know-how, they can create their own weapon. Or, instead of a detonation, they can acquire some amount of nuclear waste and threaten to render a large area uninhabitable through its release.

The Scenario

Sometime in the 2003–2006 time frame, a splinter group of the Islamic Movement of Uzbekistan (IMU) releases announcements through the world press claiming that it possesses one or more nuclear devices. Attacks in Russia, Europe, and the United States are threatened unless the United States and others release 2000 accused and convicted terrorists and all those captured during the Afghanistan conflict.

As the global community attempts to assess the credibility of the threat, pinpoint the location of the group and its claimed arsenal, and determine appropriate actions, the terrorists' deadline approaches. Two days before it arrives, Russian special forces, believing they have located the group's headquarters within Central Asia, launch an attack on the suspected site in Tajikistan. They find nothing.

The failure of the Tajikistan attack creates a government crisis, and Russian political figures and the press call for a full accounting of this unwarranted attack on foreign soil that needlessly endangered Russian military men. Moscow is paralyzed as military and political officials exchange recriminations. The next day, a nuclear explosion, believed to be caused by the detonation of a nuclear landmine, takes place on the outskirts of Nizhny Novgorod. Thousands of people are killed instantly and the effects are still being tallied when the terrorist group takes responsibility for the attack and announces that the United States and the European Union are next.

The U.S. intelligence community reports that it has pinpointed the group's location, and its arsenal, and that they are both within Russia.

Implications

If a terrorist group were to acquire the ability to threaten Russia and the world with nuclear use, Russia would almost certainly cooperate with the United States in efforts to stop it. If the terrorist group was located on Russian territory, however, Russia might have qualms about allowing U.S. forces in to assist and prefer to handle the matter on its own. Its ability to do so, on the other hand, may not be certain enough for Washington's comfort. Similarly, a lengthy period of Russian indecision could create an imperative for the United States to act, as could a split within Russia. Regional leaders, might for instance, ask for U.S. assistance even if Moscow did not. If the United States felt confident that it could prevent nuclear use and Russia could not, it might well ignore Russia's sensitivities or confusion.

The prospect of carrying out a small-scale armed operation on Russia's soil, with or without Moscow's consent, raises many issues. The use and condition of existing facilities is only one challenge that would face U.S. forces. Local attitudes toward Russia, the United States, and the terrorist group; the breakdown of loyalties in the area; and the capabilities of Russian military and police forces and their potential to assist or hinder operations are just a few of the critical unknowns. There is then the question of how Russia and/or the United States should retaliate.

If the United States chose to act, the sheer size of the Russian landmass, combined with the need for operational speed, would place much of the burden on the U.S. Air Force. There would simply be no other way to reach most potential targets. The U.S. Air Force might also be engaged in other operations to ameliorate the consequences of any nuclear explosion. Regardless of what action is taken, there seems little question that the United States would be involved in such a scenario. It engages core U.S. interests and would create a real imperative for the United States to act.

WAR IN THE CAUCASUS

The prospect of something going terribly wrong in the Caucasus—an area that the U.S. government has described as vital to its national interests—is often raised, and for good reason. The United States and Russia support competing plans for the exploitation of Caspian energy resources and their export through the Caucasus region. The United States supports natural gas and oil pipeline routes transiting Azerbaijan, Georgia, and Turkey. Russia has opposed these plans and would simply expand existing routes through its territory.[2] See Figure 8.2.

While Armenia remains loyal to Moscow, Georgia and Azerbaijan have made clear their desire to develop and deepen their friendships with NATO and the United States into a real alignment. Along with Ukraine, they have formed the core of a post-Soviet grouping that seeks to gain increased independence from Moscow. Among other things, they have formed a joint peacekeeping battalion, and one of the battalion's planned tasks will be to ensure the security of pipeline routes through Georgia and Azerbaijan.

Overall, NATO cooperation with Georgia and Azerbaijan is similar to NATO activities with other Partnership for Peace (PfP) states. NATO ally Turkey, however, has been particularly active in assisting the two PfP states and, to a large extent, sponsoring their participation in the program and in peacekeeping in the former Yugoslavia. Turkey's motivations hinge on its hopes for energy resources in the region, although ethnic, religious, and linguistic ties with Azerbaijan may also be said to play a role.

---

[2]Russia and Turkey have also been cooperating to develop a natural gas route from the former to the latter, with pipeline to be laid underneath the Black Sea. It should also be noted that in recent months Russia has exhibited a more cooperative attitude in regard to a range of pipeline routes including ones it previously opposed.

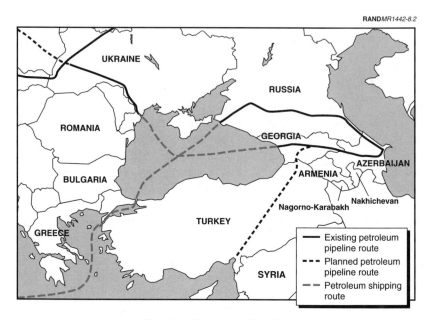

RAND*MR1442-8.2*

Fig. 8.2—Caucasus Pipelines

Russia has seen efforts by NATO and Turkey in the region as un-abashed poaching in its area of interest and influence, and has re-peatedly warned Georgia and Azerbaijan against aligning themselves too closely with the West, although it has tempered its attitude since September 11, even as the United States has stepped up its activities in the region. It has also been reluctant to agree to the final withdrawal of all of its military forces from Georgia, where several units remain based and where Russian peacekeepers continue to serve in the more unstable secessionist regions of that republic. Russia has repeatedly accused Georgia and Azerbaijan of assisting rebels in Chechnya.

The Scenario

The situation in the region remains unstable following the comple-tion of the Baku-Tbilisi-Ceyhan and Transcaspian pipelines for ex-port of Caspian natural gas and oil to Europe through the Caucasus and Turkey. Russian troops remain in Georgia, ostensibly in a peacekeeping capacity, and both Abkhazia and South Ossetia retain hopes of separating from Georgia. U.S. military trainers are no longer in Georgia, but contingents of Turkish forces remain in Georgia and Azerbaijan.

In Russia, too, the situation remains unsettled, as Russian occupation of the separatist Chechen province is marked by sporadic firefights and terrorist attacks throughout Russia. The most recent accusations by Russia that Azerbaijan and Georgia are providing aid and comfort to Chechen rebels is met by a counterclaim that Russian troops are supplying arms to separatist groups within Georgia. As the war of words escalates, Russia shifts more troops to the Georgian border, as well as some toward Azerbaijan.

Ukraine announces its intent to fully support Georgia and Azerbaijan even as reports surface of terrorist attacks on the pipelines that traverse Georgia in the south, carrying oil and natural gas to Turkey. Ukraine reinforces its contribution to the joint peacekeeping battalion it has formed with Georgia and Azerbaijan to protect the pipelines. Armenian troops move north toward the border with Azerbaijan and there are renewed clashes in Nagorno-Karabakh. Nakhichevan, a region of Azerbaijan that shares no common border with it, asks the central government to dispatch forces to protect it from a possible Armenian invasion.

After clashes between Russian troops in Georgia and units of the Georgia-Ukraine-Azerbaijan peacekeeping force, Russia claims that its units were acting independently of central command. However, the clashes continue, and a terrorist attack on the pipelines significantly slows the flow of oil into Turkey and spills enough oil to create an environmental hazard.

Ukraine, Azerbaijan, and Georgia at this point appeal to NATO for consultations, a right they have as PfP states. During the NATO consultations, Turkey argues that a NATO peacekeeping force should be dispatched to the region.

Implications

Energy interests, allied involvement, and a history of commitment to the region would create real incentives for the United States to take action in this situation. Unfavorable Russian response to U.S. activities in its backyard and the long-term effects on U.S.-Russian relations would constitute serious disincentives.

Military operations in the Caucasus, with or without Russian cooperation, would be extremely challenging. Moreover, guarding and protecting the pipelines would be exceedingly difficult. In highly forested and mountainous terrain, pipeline routes follow roads and waterways, which make it nearly impossible to distinguish between ordinary traffic and the movement of enemy forces.

Facilities in this region, particularly in Georgia, are on the whole in poorer condition than those in Russia, although there are numerous military bases in the area. There are many separatist enclaves in the Caucasus, and the support of local populations cannot be counted on. Nuclear waste depositories and a nuclear power plant in Armenia are other things to be concerned about. If these should get into the line of fire or be captured by hostile forces, environmental catastrophe could result.

Leaving aside the possibility of having to engage Russian forces, there are ways to limit U.S. involvement in this scenario. Because Turkey is already part of the mix and is agitating for NATO participation, there is no reason that Ankara cannot provide the bulk of whatever NATO force is dispatched. Still, the United States and other allies might find themselves forced to send in some troops of their own, if only to demonstrate commitment. If this is the case, it is almost certain that U.S. Air Force assets would be part of the force mix.

This scenario is plausible and it involves key U.S. interests including its NATO allies and Caspian energy resources. Furthermore, it is reasonable that events in the Caucasus will evolve in such a way that U.S. military assistance will be requested by one or another of the parties. As always, it will remain Washington's decision whether to act.

SCENARIO IMPLICATIONS

Several conclusions appear to follow the scenarios described above. First, few scenarios are truly likely to evolve into situations where the United States has little choice but to act, especially in the near term.

Second, it is unlikely that the United States will act without Russian support or at least acquiescence, although it is certainly possible to conceive of scenarios where it would be tempting to do so. Moreover, depending on how the center-periphery relationship develops, even a "welcomed" U.S. response could come up against opposition if the wrong group issues the invitation.

It is also clear that while probabilities may not be all that high, risks are, and key U.S. interests are affected by what goes on in and near Russia. The sheer size of Russia and its geography will almost certainly necessitate the use of Air Force assets in any U.S. action in the region. This means that the United States, and the U.S. Air Force, must be prepared for a range of operations in this part of the world, even as they hope that none of the missions outlined here ever come to pass.

Chapter Nine

NEXT STEPS: PLANNING FOR AND PREVENTING CONTINGENCIES

PLANNING FOR CONTINGENCIES

None of the scenarios outlined in the previous chapter, nor indeed any of the myriad others that could be imagined, ask the United States or its Air Force to do anything either is not capable of doing. The discrete tasks involved—transport, security, peace enforcement, logistical support, reconnaissance, and command, control, communications, and intelligence (C3I)—are all things that the Air Force does frequently and does well. To the casual observer, this would suggest that no matter how bad things get in Russia, the United States need not worry. If it has to get involved, it should have no problems accomplishing whatever tasks are required.

However, the ability to perform tasks in one operational environment does not necessarily translate into equal facility with the same missions in a different environment. The Russian setting presents unique and serious challenges. Many of the same events that increase the probability of the need for U.S. intervention will also make that intervention more operationally challenging. The uncertain and largely unknown state of the infrastructure at Russian airfields and air bases, the uncertain nature of local military and civilian response, and varying attitudes among Russians toward their own government and toward the United States combine with geographical constraints of distance, terrain, and weather conditions to create a challenging and unpredictable environment. Even without the factors of Russia's deterioration, a simple look at a map showing likely areas of conflict—the Urals, the Caucasus, and the Far East—reveals parts of the world that are difficult to reach and operate in. The fact that the other constraints are also very much in evidence creates an imperative to plan well in advance.

What does the Air Force need to know before it can effectively deploy to this region? Key considerations include:

- **What could happen?** Developing potential scenarios requires an understanding of what states and substate actors might be involved and how they might affect U.S. Air Force operations. Knowledge of the terrain and the geography is no less critical.

- **What would be needed?** What tools, facilities, equipment, and coalition partners would be required in each possible scenario? How readily available are they? If the right tools were unavailable, what might serve as adequate substitutes?

- **What could go wrong?** How could the operational environment frustrate U.S. operations both in the planning stages and once under way? How can the U.S. Air Force protect its people and equipment in the theater against likely threats? What is likely to constrain operations and how can it be dealt with?

- **How could these and other problems be prevented and mitigated?** Planning ahead is the first key to effective crisis response, but having a wide range of contingency plans is also essential. No matter what the United States and its Air Force plan for, what actually comes to pass will be different. However, if there are a number of alternative responses available, some combination of them, with a little modification, may very well fit the situation that emerges.

This sort of contingency planning for most regions of the world is commonly carried out by military staffs at the relevant regional command. This makes sense; because their forces would carry out the mission, they should be the one to plan for it. In the case of Russia, however, the regional unified commands that would most likely have operational responsibility (European Command [EUCOM], Pacific Command [PACOM]), or, perhaps, Central Command (CENTCOM), have until very recently lacked the mandate for detailed planning along these lines.

No U.S. regional command was authorized to undertake extensive planning with regard to Russia throughout the first decade of its independence because Russia was not assigned by the Unified Command Plan to the Area of Responsibility (AOR) of any of the regional commanders-in-chief (CINCs). Instead, responsibility for Russia rested with the chairman of the Joint Chiefs of Staff and the Joint Staff. The reasons were rooted in Russia's status as a nuclear power as well as in the difficulties of assigning this sprawling landmass to any regional command. As a by-product of this policy, however, little operational planning in recent years even touched upon the possibility of U.S. forces carrying out tasks in or near Russia itself.[1]

Because Russia was not in any of the regional CINCs' AORs, their planners were unlikely to take the initiative in thinking about the region without express direction from Washington. Because no such direction was forthcoming, the regional commands did not have assets allocated to planning or preparing for Russia-oriented missions.

Although planners in U.S. Air Force Europe (USAFE), EUCOM, and their PACOM counterparts were not charged with planning for operations within Russia, they were authorized to develop and implement military-to-military contacts with the Russian armed forces. To a large extent, these contacts are the single most significant component of the U.S. military's day-to-day "shaping" activities with Russia. It is hoped that through such military engagement, the potential for conflict will be reduced and the conditions for effective cooperation created. In addition to their shaping role, U.S.-Russian military-to-military engagement activities are essential to gathering the information necessary to plan for possible contingencies in and near Russia.

---

[1]Author discussions with EUCOM and Joint Staff personnel. There are exceptions. As already noted, FEMA has a long-standing and robust program of cooperation with its Russian counterpart EMERCOM. Their program of joint work has included joint exercises and planning for cooperative disaster mitigation and is similar in many ways to successful military-to-military relationships run by the U.S. armed forces. Furthermore, although there is no existing operational requirement to do so, an effort continues to collect the sort of data that would be useful for such planning should it become necessary. For instance, U.S. Air Force personnel are consistent in seeking airfield information at all opportunities, such as military-to-military contacts, Cooperative Threat Reduction (CTR) weapons dismantlement and inspections, and so forth.

Russia has now been assigned to the EUCOM AOR. To some extent, this will ameliorate many problems. It will also, however, raise new concerns. Russia's critical importance to U.S. policy means that organizations and individuals who have previously had planning responsibility for Russia—the chairman of the Joint Chiefs of Staff and the Joint Staff—will retain a prominent voice in how EUCOM approaches Russia. Moreover, the history of engagement by other regional commands, particularly PACOM, raises questions as to how engagement activities with Russia in the Pacific theater will be coordinated from Europe—and how plans for missions involving Asian Russia will be developed. It seems likely that EUCOM, PACOM, CENTCOM, and their component commands will all need to plan and prepare for contingency responses in and around Russia. They will need to work together to develop and implement game plans for taking advantage of cooperative activities with Russia and other neighbors to gather crucial information and build habits of joint cooperation. Such habits will prove enormously useful should crises of the type discussed here emerge. They also need the organizational authority to coordinate this planning, under the guidance of the Joint Chiefs of Staff and the office of the Secretary of Defense. Any and all of these regional commands could ultimately develop and execute the crisis response. It is imperative that each has the opportunity and adequate resources to plan for such operations.

PREVENTING CONTINGENCIES

Russian-U.S. military-to-military contacts can help to mitigate some of the factors of Russia's decline and prevent crisis contingencies from emerging. Unfortunately, this sort of cooperation has hit a great many roadblocks in recent years. The current level of military-to-military contacts quite simply precludes the sort of cooperation necessary to achieve such goals. Russia has on various occasions abruptly pulled back from contacts and has made it difficult (or impossible) for U.S. personnel to gain access to its bases and facilities, preventing them from ascertaining their condition and capacity.

The reasons for the Russian attitude are complex, but they are rooted in Russian perceptions of U.S. attitudes and foreign policy toward their country. From the Russian perspective, throughout the mid- and late 1990s Washington missed no opportunity to demonstrate its greater strength and to embarrass Moscow. Again and again, the Russians were reminded that they were not the great power they once were, as the United States pursued policies—in the former Yugoslavia, in Central Asia and the Caucasus, in Central and Eastern Europe, and in developing a national missile defense—that the Russians made clear were anathema to them. Reflecting the very weakness they so abhor, the Russians had limited options available to them to demonstrate their discontent and to punish the United States. Cutting back on cooperative ties was one of the few actions they could take to signal their displeasure to Washington. Unfortunately (certainly for Russia and very possibly for the United States), that has not been sufficient incentive for the United States to reverse its policies, and many contacts and channels of communication have been shut down. From Washington's perspective, there was little reason to humor Russia through policy compromises when Moscow could muster no immediate threat to U.S. interests or behavior.

The situation was exacerbated by the burgeoning relationships between the U.S. military and other independent successor states to the USSR. Russia's general unwillingness to cooperate to date has resulted in a strengthened focus on its neighboring states, which are in the AORs of various regional commands and with which Washington has developed military cooperation programs. To Russia this looked even more like a concerted U.S. effort to encircle and isolate it by courting its natural allies. From the U.S. perspective, it was simply a reasonable policy to bolster the independence and modest economic reform efforts in these fledgling states. Moreover, since many of these states were willing to participate in joint exercises and contacts with the U.S. military, Washington had the opportunity to gather some key information about facilities and assets for contingency planning that it could not gather in Russia. This means that if a crisis does emerge, the United States may find that the best way of responding to events in Russia is to rely on airfields and facilities in neighboring states. Unfortunately, such an approach could further anger Russia and hamper cooperation in the crisis.

This is why it is imperative to continue to seek means to improve relations with Moscow generally and with the Russian MoD in particular, despite the many obstacles. Improved relations would be the best basis for successful and effective planning for crisis contingencies and speedy and effective responses to crises, when and if they occur. In the same way that deterioration both increases the likelihood of U.S. military involvement and ensures that this involvement will be tremendously challenging should it occur, Western efforts to help address Russia's problems in the near term will make assistance in a crisis more effective if it nonetheless becomes necessary.

The situation today, in the wake of the September 11, 2001, terrorist attacks on the United States, provides some hope for improved future relations, although the relationship with Russia must be managed carefully. True, Russia and the United States have publicly recognized their commonality of views on a number of issues, especially the global fight against terrorism. However, the fact that the two countries share a common goal does not mean that they share either their beliefs about how best to attain that goal or their definitions of terrorism, counterterrorism, and victory over terrorism. Moreover, each country continues to have its own foreign policy interests aside from (and in some cases over and above) the counterterrorist agenda. Thus, it is crucial that Washington not take for granted Russia's support and continued friendship. Rather, it should seek to build on current cooperation by demonstrating to Russia that good relations with it are key to U.S. foreign policy. In the meantime, it should take advantage of the cooperative activities that do emerge to better understand the processes of decline in Russia, both to assist in the design of mitigation strategies and to better plan for crisis should mitigation fail. It should also take these opportunities to gather the information that will be needed in the event of a military contingency in or near Russia, recognizing that a downturn in relations could limit further collection of such data.

How can the United States demonstrate to Russia that U.S.-Russian relations are a priority? President Putin's rapprochement with the United States has not met with undiluted support in Russia (some aspects of this were discussed in Chapter Six). Rather, there are elements in both official and public opinion in Russia that view the United States as making a concerted effort to usurp Russia's great power role, to weaken it in every arena, and to make it look helpless and incompetent in the process.[2] Yet, as we have discussed, the United States has in fact a clear national security preference for a stable and secure Russia over a weak and destabilized one. It is therefore very much in the U.S. interest to demonstrate this to Russia. One approach is to seek compromise with Russia, particularly where such compromise can help Russia at little cost to the United States. Another is to provide assistance in key areas. Some specific points of compromise, cooperation, and assistance include:

- The United States should continue to publicly emphasize Russia's role in the global war on terrorism, signaling that Moscow is an important partner. This will elevate Moscow's prestige and enhance the potential for future relations. Bilateral steps taken by Russia and the United States in support of the counter-terrorist effort (joint exercises, information sharing, law enforcement cooperation) should be publicized whenever possible.

- The United States and NATO should continue to take steps to improve and make more substantive Russia's cooperation with the alliance through the NATO-Russian Council and beyond. This can begin with counter-terrorism cooperation but can expand to other areas of mutual interest. The United States should also encourage NATO allies to develop their bilateral relationships with the Russians, particularly in cooperation in nonmilitary areas of mutual interest, such as law enforcement, and to contribute to efforts to improve the situation in Russia, such as through cooperative threat-reduction programs and improving nuclear reactor plant safety.

- Although the United States has decided to withdraw from the ABM treaty, cooperative development of missile defense technology with Russia is still possible. A cooperative approach in this area would clearly demonstrate that U.S. missile defense is not aimed against Moscow, emphasize respect for Russia and its technological know-how, and perhaps garner benefits for Russia's struggling military industrial complex.

---

[2]As this analysis suggests, one could well argue that Russia is accomplishing this admirably without assistance from Washington.

- Caspian oil and gas export development is another possible area of cooperation. Russian firms are deeply involved in a range of options for Caspian energy export, and this sort of multinational business cooperation should be encouraged. At the same time, the United States should also support ongoing cooperation between NATO ally Turkey and Russia to build a natural gas route from Russia to Turkey. This route appears financially and practically feasible, and supporting it would provide the United States with an excellent opportunity to bolster both Russia and Turkey.

- The United States should seek to integrate and make complementary its engagement with Russia and with other post-Soviet states, particularly now that it is becoming so much more active in Central Asia and the Caucasus. Russia has been willing to accept U.S. presence in Central Asia and the Caucasus in conjunction with the war in Afghanistan and the campaign against terrorism, although several Russian officials have made it clear that they expect the U.S. presence to be temporary. If not approached carefully, continued U.S.-military cooperation activities in this part of the world have the potential to hamper U.S.-Russian relations and contribute to instability in the region. If the United States takes a somewhat different approach, however, seeking to involve Russia in its overtures to the Central Asian and the Caucasus states and to, whenever possible, work cooperatively with Russia in engaging them, U.S.-Russian ties (and regional security) can be improved through such cooperation.

- The United States should reconsider its activities in support of economic reform in Russia and recognize the trends toward and dangers of economic regionalization. Particular attention must be paid to structural reform of legal and economic institutions. The United States should work with Russia to support foreign investment, encouraging U.S. companies to come to Russia and helping Russia to create a legal structure that will attract them.

- The United States should intensify efforts to improve nuclear safety and security in both weapons and nonweapons sectors in Russia, building on and expanding past successes such as the CTR program. It should also encourage its European allies to do the same.

- FEMA-EMERCOM cooperation should continue and serve as a model for closer ties between other organizations in the two countries, at both the federal and local level.

- The United States should seek to identify new areas of cooperation and support nascent cooperative programs. Shared interests—military roles in environmental remediation, for example—can provide an excellent basis for broader discussions and cooperation in the future.

Increasingly active involvement and friendly ties with Russia can gain and maintain for the United States the access to Russian decisionmakers it needs to have a positive influence on developments within that country by means of advice, assistance, and investment. It is possible, of course, that Moscow will refuse Washington's help. But it is certain that without engagement, there is no hope of positively affecting the situation in Russia.

Moreover, effective engagement, including but not limited to military-to-military contacts, could give the U.S. government and its military personnel the opportunity to plan with Russian counterparts for various contingencies. The organizations in question could then work together should they need to in a future crisis, and Russia's own capacity to respond effectively would be improved (U.S. planners might also learn a few things).

Finally, cooperative programs on Russian soil with Russian military and civilian organizations could provide key information on Russian capabilities, facilities, infrastructure, and geography that is essential for contingency planning. Without this information, preparation is significantly hampered. With it, it would be possible to better understand the operational environment and to prepare to operate in it if need be.

But engaging Russia, and getting and sustaining a positive Russian response, will not be easy. The United States government, including the Air Force, should be prepared to carry out contingencies in a worse-case scenario, one in which cooperation has failed and the relationship with Russia is poor. Even under such circumstances, and no matter how poor relations between Washington and Moscow might be, the United States will still need to protect its interests, and those will be affected by events in and near Russia. Thus, the United States must consider how best to do that given a combination of threatening crisis in Russia and poor relations with that country.

Chapter Ten

THE AIR FORCE ROLE

The U.S. Air Force has a role to play in the effort both to broaden cooperative ties with Russia and to assist in planning for various types of crisis response. The Air Force would undoubtedly be tasked with carrying out significant portions of such missions should they emerge. It is therefore very much in its best interests to begin identifying and thinking through possible scenarios. It is also in the Air Force's interests to ensure that it has its own ideas and approaches, which can then be factored into the planning of the regional unified command(s) with respect to Russia. In this way, the Air Force can ensure that it is well-prepared to successfully carry out any missions it might be assigned.

The U.S. Air Force should maintain its current key role in efforts to build ties with Russia, including high-level and professional exchanges, exercises, and visits. It should take the lead in working with Russian counterparts to think about possible contingencies, in Russia and globally, and how the United States and Russia can cooperate to respond to them, recognizing the primary role of air power (particularly airlift operations) in many contingencies. The Air Force should pursue the design and implementation of military exercises with its Russian counterparts in joint operational environments. One possibly fruitful area to explore might be counter-terrorist operations, perhaps in conjunction with Central Asian or South Caucasus military forces. Air Force personnel should also continue to take the opportunities presented by cooperation with Russian counterparts to hedge against future downturns in relations to gather information that will support a range of contingency planning in the future.

Along the same line, Air Force planning and preparation should continue to use intelligence assets and analysis to gather information about Russian and regional facilities (i.e., airfields, terrain) and to identify regions where crisis could occur. To do this effectively requires accurate assessments of regional military structures and capabilities as well as the condition of local military and civilian infrastructure; familiarization with local politics, including regional power groupings and the current state of center-periphery relations; and overall awareness of potential operating environments in and near Russia. Planners can then better forecast what could go wrong and better understand how to ameliorate crisis should it occur. Such information gathering and analysis may be hampered when cooperation lags, but there are other ways to gather these data, which may become vital should relations deteriorate. Under circumstances when U.S. military cooperation with Russia is vigorous, intelligence analysis that identifies potential crises can and must be effectively combined with U.S.-Russian cooperation to avert those crises.

When relations are tense and many military-to-military programs are put on hold, the Air Force should take advantage of those bilateral cooperation programs that the Russians allow to continue because of perceived gains to be had. Past examples include the Cooperative Threat Reduction Program and FEMA cooperation with EMERCOM. These activities can help shape Russia's environment while also providing information. A FEMA-EMERCOM cooperation is a prime example. FEMA should welcome Air Force involvement in its planning and thinking about Russia because it may have to rely on the Air Force to execute operations far from home. The Air Force should take advantage of FEMA's access to Russia and its organizations to better learn how events might unfold in a crisis and what its role might be.

However, a more comprehensive downturn in relations might see an end to activities. Air Force contingency planning would then have to consider how bases outside of Russia might be used to gain access to areas within it. The development of plans that assume little cooperation from Russia, and perhaps even hostility from it as U.S. forces seek to protect their country's interests in the region, would become more urgent if declining U.S.-Russian relations make such a situation more likely. Continued U.S. engagement with states on Russia's periphery helps to ensure that the United States will be able to act when and where it needs to, should an emergency arise. As the U.S. Air Force and the U.S. military as a whole approach these questions, however, they must be aware of the risks they entail.

Increased activity in and cooperation with states on Russia's periphery will stimulate Moscow's distrust of U.S. intent and could exacerbate tension in an already difficult U.S.-Russian relationship, thus making the "hedge" a self-fulfilling prophecy. Clearly, certain approaches risk creating a backlash that could jeopardize U.S. efforts to build ties with Russia. The United States, and the U.S. Air Force, should move forward very cautiously. Whenever possible, engagement with other post-Soviet states, particularly in Central Asia, should include Russia in some role, emphasizing multilateral cooperation. This would serve the local states as well, because hostile relations with their larger and more powerful neighbor are not in their best interests, whereas positive ties with both Russia and the United States are ideal.

The planning and information-gathering tasks described above will require the allocation of resources and assets. Intelligence analysis, scenario development, and planning all require trained personnel and financial support to implement. Furthermore, the Air Force cannot accomplish these tasks alone but must coordinate with appropriate staff elements of the regional commands as well as with other services. Because none of these organizations is as yet comprehensively and cooperatively engaged in such work, the Air Force might want to consider taking the lead by building on its own substantial capabilities.

In the best-case scenario, of course, the United States will be able to work with Russia to alleviate many of the problems that country faces, helping to halt and reverse the dangerous processes of decline to create a stronger and more stable Russia. The U.S. Air Force could assist in this effort by being at its forefront; it can help identify the problems and engage Russian counterparts on potential cooperative responses. No less important is the task of ensuring that the Air Force and the country are prepared for a very different outcome—a crisis in an uncooperative and unfriendly Russia, and possibly even a resistant Russia. Either way, the Air Force must have a plan of action.

SELECTED BIBLIOGRAPHY

Books

Allison, Graham T., Owen R. Coté, Jr., Richard A. Falkenrath, and Steven E. Miller, *Avoiding Nuclear Anarchy: Containing the Threat of Loose Russian Nuclear Weapons and Fissile Material*, The MIT Press, Cambridge, Massachusetts, 1996.

Åslund, Anders, *How Russia Became a Market Economy*, The Brookings Institution, Washington, DC, 1995.

Azrael, Jeremy R., and Emil A. Payin (eds.), *Conflict and Consensus in Ethno-Political and Center-Periphery Relations in Russia*, RAND, CF-139, 1998.

Blainey, Geoffrey, *The Causes of War*, The Free Press, New York, 1988 edition.

Boycko, Maxim, Andrei Shleifer, and Robert Vishny, *Privatizing Russia*, The MIT Press, Cambridge, Massachusetts, 1995.

Bradley, D. J., *Behind the Nuclear Curtain: Radioactive Waste Management in the Former Soviet Union*, Battelle Press, Columbus, Ohio, 1997.

DaVanzo, Julie, and Clifford Grammich, *Dire Demographics: Population Trends in the Russian Federation*, RAND, MR-1273-WFHF/DLPF/RF, 2001.

Fainsod, Merle, *How Russia Is Ruled,* Harvard University Press, Cambridge, Massachusetts, 1963.

Feshbach, Murray, and Alfred Friendly, Jr., *Ecocide in the USSR,* HarperCollins, New York, 1992.

Gilpin, Robert, *War and Change in World Politics,* Cambridge University Press, New York, 1981.

Hosking, Geoffrey, *The Awakening of the Soviet Union,* Harvard University Press, Cambridge, Massachusetts, 1991.

Hough, Jerry, *Soviet Leadership in Transition,* The Brookings Institution, Washington, DC, 1980.

———, *Russia and the West: Gorbachev and the Politics of Reform,* Simon and Schuster, New York, 1990.

Joseph, S. Nye, Jr., *Bound to Lead: The Changing Nature of American Power,* Basic Books, New York, 1990.

Oliker, Olga, *Russia's Chechen Wars: Lessons from Urban Combat,* RAND, MR-1289-A, 2001.

Organski, A.F.K., *World Politics,* 2nd ed., Knopf, New York, 1968.

Treisman, Daniel S., *After the Deluge: Regional Crises and Political Consolidation in Russia,* The University of Michigan Press, Ann Arbor, Michigan, 2001.

Walt, Stephen M., *Revolution and War,* Cornell University Press, Ithaca and London, 1996.

Wolfsthal, Jon Brook, Cristina-Astrid Chuen, and Emily Ewell Daughtry (eds.), *Nuclear Status Report: Nuclear Weapons, Fissile Material, and Export Controls in the Former Soviet Union,* Monterey Institute of International Studies and Carnegie Endowment for International Peace, Monterey, California, and Washington, DC, 2001.

Woodruff, David, *Money Unmade: Barter and the Fate of Russian Capitalism,* Cornell University Press, Ithaca and London, 1999.

Papers and Articles

Alexseev, Mikhail, "The Chinese Are Coming: Public Opinion and Threat Perception in the Russian Far East," Program on New Approaches to Russian Security (PONARS), Center for Strategic and International Studies, Washington, DC, 2001.

———, "Decentralization Versus State Collapse: Explaining Russia's Endurance," *Journal of Peace Research*, Vol. 38, No. 1, January 2001, pp. 101–106.

———, "Russia's Periphery in the Global Arena: Do Regions Matter in the Kremlin's Foreign Policy?" PONARS, 2000.

———, "The Unintended Consequences of Anti-Federalist Centralization in Russia," PONARS, 2000.

Baev, Pavel, "President Putin and His Generals: Bureaucratic Control and War-Fighting Culture," PONARS, 2001.

———, "Putin's Court: How the Military Fits In," PONARS, 2000.

Benn, David Wedgewood, "Review Article: Warm Words and Harsh Advice: A Critique of the West's Role in Russian Reforms," *International Affairs*, Vol. 77, No. 4, 2001, pp. 947–955. Benn reviews *The Tragedy of Russia's Reforms: Market Bolshevism Against Democracy* by Peter Reddaway and Dmitri Glinski; *Failed Crusade: America and the Tragedy of Post-Communist Russia* by Stephen F. Cohen; and *The New Russia: Transition Gone Awry* by Lawrence R. Klein and Marshall Pomer (eds.).

Blair, Bruce, and Clifford G. Gaddy, "Russia's Aging War Machine," *Brookings Review*, Summer 1999, pp. 10–13.

Bozh'eva, Olga, "Exercises: Commonwealth–2001," *Armeiskii Sbornik*, No. 10, October 2001, pp. 30–33.

Breslauer, George, Josef Brada, Clifford G. Gaddy, Richard Ericson, Carol Saivetz, and Victor Winston, "Russia at the End of Yel'tsin's Presidency," *Post-Soviet Affairs*, Vol. 16, No. 1, 2000, pp. 1–32.

Cimbala, Stephen J., "Russia's Nuclear Command and Control: Mission Malaise," *The Journal of Slavic Military Studies*, Vol. 14, No. 2, June 2001, pp. 1–28.

David, Steven R., "Saving America from the Coming Civil Wars," *Foreign Affairs*, Vol. 78, No. 1, Winter 1999, pp. 103–116.

Eberstadt, Nicholaas, "Russia: Too Sick to Matter?" *Policy Review*, June/July 1999, No. 95, pp. 3–22.

Evangelista, Matthew, "Russia's Path to a New Regional Policy," PONARS, 2000.

Gaddy, Clifford G., and Barry W. Ickes, "Russia's Virtual Economy," *Foreign Affairs*, Vol. 77, No. 5, September/October 1998, pp. 53–67.

———, "The Virtual Economy and Economic Recovery in Russia," *Transition Newsletter*, Vol. 12, No. 1, February–March 2001.

Galeotti, Mark, "Russia's Criminal Army," *Jane's Intelligence Review*, Vol. 11, No. 6, June 1999, pp. 8–10.

Gel'man, Vladimir, "The Rise and Fall of Federal Reform in Russia," PONARS, 2001.

Gerber, Theodore, "Russia's Population Crisis: The Migration Dimension," PONARS, 2000.

———, "The Development of Self-Employment in Russia," PONARS, 2001.

Hale, Henry, "The State of Democratization in Russia in Light of the Elections," PONARS, 2000.

Helman, Gerald, and Steven R. Ratner, "Saving Failed States," *Foreign Policy*, No. 89, Winter 1992–1993.

Herd, Graeme P., "Russia: Systemic Transformation or Federal Collapse?" *Journal of Peace Research*, Vol. 36, No. 3, 1999, pp. 259–269.

Herrera, Yoshiko M., "Attempts Under Putin to Create a Unified Economic Space in Russia," PONARS, 2001.

Kipp, Jacob W., "Russia's Nonstrategic Nuclear Weapons," *Military Review*, May–June 2001.

Kosals, L., "The shadow economy as an attribute of Russian capitalism" (in Russian), *Voprosy Ekonomiki*, No. 10, 1998, pp. 59–60.

Kotz, David M., "Is Russia Becoming Capitalist," *Science and Society*, Vol. 65, No. 2, Summer 2001, pp. 157–181.

Kozlov, Viktor, "Point of view: Don't joke with airpower" (in Russian), *Armeiskii Sbornik*, No. 10, October 2001, pp. 8–10.

Kramer, Mark, "Capital Flight and Russian Economic Reform," PONARS, 2000.

Lehman, Susan Goodrich, "Inter-Ethnic Conflict in the Republics of Russia in Light of Religious Revival," *Post-Soviet Geography and Economics*, Vol. 39, No. 8, 1998, pp. 461–493.

Levshin, V. I., A. V. Nedelin, and Mikhail Sosnovskiy, "Use of nuclear weapons to de-escalate military operations" (in Russian), *Voennaiia Mysl*, No. 3, May–June 1999, pp. 34–37.

Liberman, Peter, "The Spoils of Conquest," *International Security*, Vol. 18, No. 2, Fall 1993, pp. 125–153.

Mansfield, Edward D., and Jack Snyder, "Democratization and the Danger of War," *International Security*, Vol. 20, No. 1, Summer 1995, pp. 5–38.

Medvedev, V., "Problems of Russia's Economic Security," *Russian Social Science Review*, Vol. 39, No. 6, November–December 1998, p. 18.

Nicholson, Martin, "Putin's Russia: Slowing the Pendulum Without Stopping the Clock," *International Affairs*, Vol. 77, No. 3, 2001, pp. 867–884.

Ozerov, Viktor, "Point of view: Whose finger should be on the pulse?" (in Russian), *Armeiskii Sbornik*, No. 3, March 2001, pp. 4–7.

Payin, Emil A., "Ethnic Separatism," in Jeremy R. Azrael and Emil A. Payin (eds.), *Conflict and Consensus in Ethno-Political and Center-Periphery Relations in Russia*, RAND, CF-139, 1998, p. 17.

Petrov, Nikolai, "Policization Versus Democratization," PONARS, 2001.

Podvig, Pavel, "Russian Nuclear Forces in Ten Years With and Without START II," PONARS, 1999.

Popov, Vladimir, "Exchange Rate Policy After the Currency Crisis: Walking the Tightrope," PONARS, 2000.

———, "Reform Strategies and Economic Performance of Russia's Regions," *World Development*, Vol. 29, No. 5, 2001, pp. 865–886.

———, "Why the Russian Economy Is Unlikely to Become a New 'Asian Tiger,'" PONARS, 2000.

Potter, William C., and Fred L. Wehling, "Sustainability: A Vital Component of Nuclear Material Security in Russia," *The Nonproliferation Review*, Vol. 7, No. 1, Spring 2000.

Radaev, V., "On the role of force in Russian business relationships" (in Russian), *Voprosy Ekonomiki*, No. 10, October 1998, pp. 81–100.

Radaev, Vadim, "Consolidation of the Russian State and Economic Policy Scenarios Under Putin," PONARS, 2000.

Radovanyi, Jean, "And What If Russia Breaks Up?" *Post-Soviet Geography*, Vol. 33, June 1992, pp. 69–77.

Safavian, Mehnaz S., Douglas H. Graham, and Claudio Gonzalez-Vega, "Corruption and Microenterprises in Russia," *World Development*, Vol. 29, No. 7, 2001, pp. 1215–1224.

Simonenko, Aleksandr, and Roman Tovstik, "Ordered to survive" (in Russian), *Armeiskii Sbornik*, No. 10, October 2001, pp. 41–44.

Sokov, Nikolai, "The Reality and Myths of Nuclear Regionalism in Russia," PONARS, 2000.

Solnik, Steve, "The New Federal Structure: More Centralized or More of the Same?" PONARS, 2000.

———, "Putin and the Provinces," PONARS, 2000.

Stoner-Weiss, Kathryn, "The Limited Reach of Russia's Party System: Under-Institutionalization in the Provinces," PONARS, 2000.

Taylor, Brian, "The Duma and Military Reform," PONARS, 2000.

——, "Putin and the Military: How Long Will the Honeymoon Last?" PONARS, 2000.

Tuminez, Astrid, "Russian Nationalism and Vladimir Putin's Russia," PONARS, 2000.

Weslowsky, Tony, "Risky Business," *Bulletin of the Atomic Scientists*, Vol. 57, No. 3, May/June 2001, pp. 40–44.

Woodruff, David, "Too Much of a Good Thing? High Oil Prices and Russian Monetary Policy," PONARS, 2000.

Yankov, Aleksandr, Igor' Zadorozhniy, and Vadim Vinnik, "Prevention of 'barracks crime'" (in Russian), *Armeiskii Sbornik*, March 2000.

Yost, David S., "Russia's Non-Strategic Nuclear Forces," *International Affairs*, Vol. 77, No. 3, 2001, pp. 531–551.

Monographs and Reports

Center for Nonproliferation Studies at the Monterey Institute of International Studies and the Non-Proliferation Project at the Carnegie Endowment for International Peace, *Nuclear Successor States of the Soviet Union: Status Report on Nuclear Weapons, Fissile Material and Export Controls*, No. 5, March 1998, http://cns.miis.edu/pubs/reports/statrep.htm, pp. 105–110.

Charlick-Paley, Tanya, "Accommodating to the Loss of Empire: Is There a Post-Imperial Military Syndrome?" Ph.D. Dissertation, Ohio State University, 1997, pp. 170–175.

Country Analysis Brief: Russia [Internet], Energy Information Agency, U.S. Department of Energy, October 2001 [cited February 23, 2002]. Available from http://www.eia.doe.gov/emeu/cabs/russia.html.

Gaddy, Clifford G., and Barry William Ickes, *Stability and Disorder: An Evolutionary Analysis of Russia's Virtual Economy*, The Davidson Institute, 1999.

Graham, Thomas, and Arnold Horelick, *U.S.-Russian Relations at the Turn of the Century*, Report of the U.S. Working Group on U.S.-Russian Relations, Carnegie Endowment for International Peace, Washington, DC, May, 2000.

Human Rights Watch, *World Report 1999* and *World Report 2000*.

Olshansky, D. V., *Alternative Scenarios of the Disintegration of the Russian Federation*, Potomac Foundation, McLean, Virginia, 1993.

Ovtcharova, Lilia, "What Kind of Poverty Alleviation Policy Does Russia Need?" Russian-European Centre for Economic Policy, Moscow, 2001.

Safranchuk, Ivan, *The Future of the Russian Nuclear Arsenal*, Study Paper No. 10, PIR Center, Moscow, 1999.

Source Book: Soviet-Designed Nuclear Power Plants in Russia, Ukraine, Lithuania, Armenia, the Czech Republic, the Slovak Republic, Hungary and Bulgaria, Nuclear Energy Institute, Washington, DC, 1997, p. 105.

Turbiville, Graham H., Jr., *Mafia in Uniform: The Criminalization of the Russian Armed Forces*, Foreign Military Studies Office, Fort Leavenworth, Kansas, 1995 (www.call.army.mil/call/fmso/fmsopubs/issues/mafia.htm).

U.S. General Accounting Office, *Nuclear Nonproliferation: Limited Progress in Improving Nuclear Material Security in Russia and the Newly Independent States*, GAO/RCED/NSIAD-00-82, 1982.

_____, *Nuclear Nonproliferation: Security of Russia's Nuclear Material Improving; Further Enhancements Needed*, GAO-01-312, no date.

_____, *Nuclear Safety: Concerns with the Continuing Operation of Soviet-Designed Nuclear Power Reactors*, GAO/RCED-00-97, 1997.

_____, *Weapons of Mass Destruction: Reducing the Threat from the Former Soviet Union*, Letter Report, GAO/NSIAD-95-7, October 6, 1994.

Wedel, Janine R., "U.S. Assistance for Market Reforms: Foreign Aid Failures in Russia and the Former Soviet Bloc," Cato Institute, Washington, DC, 1999.

Newspapers, Magazines, Press Services, News Digests (including internet based)

Christian Science Monitor

Foreign Broadcast Information Service

Gazeta.ru

The Independent

Interfax

ITAR-TASS

Itogi

Izvestiya

Jamestown Foundation Monitor

Johnson's Russia List

Krasnaya Zvezda

Los Angeles Times

Moscow Times

Nezavisimaya Gazeta

Nezavisimoye Voyennoye Obozreniye

The Observer (UK)

Obshchaya Gazeta

Russkii Telegraf

RFE/RL Newsline

Segodnya

Trud

Vecherniy Cheliabinsk

Vesti.ru

Wall Street Journal Europe

Washington Post

Web Sites (other than news digests) and Databases

Bellona Foundation: www.bellona.no

Digital Freedom Network: www.dfn.org

Emerging Markets Database

Institute of Freedom: Moscow Libertarium: www.libertarium.ru.

Prava.org: www.prava.org

Stratfor: www.stratfor.com

World Nuclear Association: www.world-nuclear.org

Author Discussions and Interviews

Dmitri Trenin, Ivan Safranchuk, Anatoliy Diakov, Paul Podvig, Robert North, Mikhail Ivanovich Miroshnichenko (Deputy Chief of the Nuclear and Radiation Safety Department, GosAtomNadzor) and other U.S. and Russian officials and specialists.